the CSIRO total wellbeing diet book 2

Associate Professor Manny Noakes is the stream leader for the Diet and Lifestyle program at CSIRO Human Nutrition, a multidisciplinary team of nutritionists, psychologists and exercise physiologists engaged in developing innovative programs for improving healthy lifestyle behaviour among Australians. Manny also manages clinical trials that provide scientific evidence for the efficacy of diet and exercise programs on health. Manny has published over 100 scientific papers, with a major emphasis on diet composition, weight-loss and cardiovascular health. She is a senior lecturer in the School of Medicine, Flinders University, affiliate senior lecturer in the Department of Obstetrics and Gynaecology, University of Adelaide, and affiliate associate professor in the Department of Medicine, University of Adelaide.

Professor Peter Clifton is the scientific director for clinical nutrition, obesity and related conditions at CSIRO Human Nutrition. He is also professor of medicine at the University of Adelaide, and practises as an endocrinologist at the Royal Adelaide Hospital and the Flinders Medical Centre. Peter is a frequent and sought-after speaker at national and international conferences and is also widely published in the areas of diet, functional foods and heart health. His personal research interests are diet, obesity, cardiovascular disease, and optimal diets for people with insulin resistance and diabetes.

The Commonwealth Scientific and Industrial Research Organisation (CSIRO), Australia's national science agency, has been dedicated to the practical application of knowledge and science for society and industry since 1928, and today ranks in the top one per cent of world scientific institutions in twelve out of twenty-two research fields. CSIRO Human Nutrition conducts research into human health, including disease prevention, diagnosis and innovative treatment. CSIRO Human Nutrition is also a centre of Food Science Australia, the country's largest and most diversified food and nutrition research organisation, and a joint venture between CSIRO and the Victorian Government.

www.csiro.au

PENGUIN

MICHAEL
JOSEPH

the CSIRO total wellbeing diet

book

2

dr manny noakes **with** dr peter clifton

PENGUIN
MICHAEL
JOSEPH

CSIRO

PENGUIN BOOKS

Published by the Penguin Group
Penguin Books Ltd, 80 Strand, London WC2R 0RL, England
Penguin Group (USA) Inc. 375 Hudson Street, New York, New York 10014, USA
Penguin Group (Canada), 90 Eglinton Avenue East, Suite 700, Toronto ON M4P 2Y3, Canada
(a division of Pearson Penguin Canada Inc.)
Penguin Ireland, 25 St Stephen's Green, Dublin 2, Ireland (a division of Penguin Books Ltd)
Penguin Group (Australia), 250 Camberwell Road,
Camberwell, Victoria 3124, Australia (a division of Pearson Australia Group Pty Ltd)
Penguin Books India Pvt Ltd, 11 Community Centre,
Panchsheel Park, New Delhi – 110 017, India
Penguin Group (NZ), 67 Apollo Drive, Mairangi Bay,
Auckland 1310, New Zealand (a division of Pearson New Zealand Ltd)
Penguin Books (South Africa) (Pty) Ltd, 24 Sturdee Avenue,
Rosebank, Johannesburg 2196, South Africa

Penguin Books Ltd, Registered Offices: 80 Strand, London WC2R 0RL, England

www.penguin.com

First published by Penguin Group (Australia), a division of Pearson Australia Group Pty Ltd, 2006

First published in the UK by Michael Joseph (a division of Penguin Books), 2007

1

Text copyright © CSIRO 2006

The authors would like to thank the National Heart Foundation of Australia for permission to reproduce the National Heart Foundation Tick on page 23; and the Commonwealth of Australia for permission to reproduce the data in the table on page 219, originally published in *Nutrient Reference Values for Australia and New Zealand*, by the National Health and Medical Research Council, © Commonwealth of Australia 2006.

The following brand names used in this book are registered trade marks of the following companies: All-Bran and Kellogg's All-Bran (page 8) – Kellogg Company; Bonox (page 9) and Vegemite (pages 9, 77, 81, 95) – Kraft Foods Limited; Bovril (page 9) – Conopco, Inc.; Equal (pages 206, 209, 210, 212, 220) – Merisant Company 2, SARL; Fibre Plus (pages 5, 8) – The Uncle Tobys Company Limited; Früche (pages 32, 112, 113) – National Foods Dairy Foods Limited; Ryvita (page 8) – George Weston Foods Limited; Weet-Bix (pages 8, 184) – Australasian Conference Association Limited. Kellogg's Sultana Bran (page 8) is also a trade mark of Kellogg Company.

The moral right of the authors has been asserted

Design based on an original design by Nikki Townsend © Penguin Group (Australia)
Photographs on pages v (bottom), 24, 74 and 100–213 © Ian Wallace; photographs on pages v (middle), 6, 45 and 60–73 © Steven Murray; photographs on pages 47–50 and 98 © Tim de Neefe
Food styling by Louise Pickford; food preparation by Jennifer Tolhurst and Andrew De Sousa
Recipes by Heidi Flett, except Bircher Muesli with Bran and Bran Muffins (page 116) and Baked Banana with Flaked Almonds and Grand Marnier (page 212), which are by Manny Noakes
Exercise plan by Dr Grant Brinkworth
Information on salt intake by Jennifer Keogh
Typeset in Frutiger by Post Pre-press Group, Brisbane, Queensland
Colour reproduction by Splitting Image, Clayton, Victoria
Printed in China through the Australian Book Connection

ISBN 978–0–718–15152–2

acknowledgements

We would particularly like to acknowledge Susan McLeish and Nicola Young for their patience and tireless efforts in making this book beautiful, practical and readable!

At CSIRO, thanks to Dr Atul Kacker, Dr Anthos Yannakou and the Board of Food Science Australia for their support for a follow-on to our first book.

A special thanks to Felicity Vallence, Daniel Ruffino, Julie Gibbs and Robert Sessions, for their enthusiasm and encouragement.

Finally a big thank you to the Australian public and all those who have contacted us to let us know how much the CSIRO Total Wellbeing Diet has made a difference to their lives.

CSIRO gratefully acknowledges all those who have contributed to the funding of research on higher-protein diets for weight management: CSIRO Human Nutrition; Dairy Australia; Goodman Fielder; Meat and Livestock Australia; The National Heart Foundation; The National Centre of Excellence for Functional Foods; The National Health and Medical Research Council.

contents

introduction

How to lose weight has always been a popular topic of discussion, but that's even more the case since *Book One* of the CSIRO Total Wellbeing Diet was launched. By the time this second book hits the shelves, over half a million Australians will have a copy of the first book in their possession. This fact has stunned and surprised all of us at CSIRO, but has also given us a sense of the value of our science to the average Australian. We have received countless congratulatory emails telling great success stories, and with many suggestions for future publications. Hopefully the Diet has enthused and inspired many to get healthier and fitter and to make the most of their lives. The feedback from our readers has helped us to understand which issues we needed to clarify, what we needed to describe in more detail and what extra information we needed to include in this book.

The questions and answers we have included here (see pages 29–38) will give you a taste of the wide cross-section of enquiries we had from our readers. Many of you asked for more great recipes, and we don't think you'll be disappointed with the delicious selection we've put together.

Let's face it, all that talk about good nutrition is fine, but most of us just want to cut to the chase and find out how to eat well. The menu plans were extraordinarily popular, as were the shopping lists, which took all the hard work out of preparing healthy meals. This time we've also included some more economical dishes, since some cuts of high-protein foods such as lean red meat and fish can be quite costly. If only we could help you with the cleaning up as well . . .

One of the hardest things about weight-loss is finding inspiration and motivation. That you've bought this book shows that you're on the right track. In it we've tried to provide some shortcuts to help you get started easily and make your weight-loss program a breeze.

the controversy:
are the critics right?

Since nutrition scientists are constantly making new discoveries, we need to revise our recommendations for healthy eating from time to time. However, nutrition is an art as well as a science. It's an art because it requires creativity

to develop a healthy eating plan for people who differ in their food preferences, beliefs and culture, let alone in their nutritional needs according to their genes and life stage. As we discover more about how our genes and our environment interact, it's becoming increasingly difficult to provide a single set of dietary recommendations that will be suitable for everyone.

What we do know is that there is more than one approach to healthy eating. For example, although this book focuses on a high-protein eating plan, it is also possible to lose weight healthily with a high-carbohydrate or a vegetarian eating pattern. What is important is what works for you.

Our books focus on the CSIRO Total Wellbeing Diet because this eating plan is based on our recent scientific studies, as well as those of researchers overseas. However, CSIRO has also created and published a high-carbohydrate eating plan called the 12345+ Diet (see www.csiro.au/ 12345). The *Dietary Guidelines for Australian Adults*, produced by the National Health and Medical Research Council, provide general information on a similarly high-carbohydrate eating style. The *Australian Guide to Healthy Eating*, produced for the Commonwealth Department of Health and Family Services, is also helpful if you prefer a diet lower in animal protein and higher in carbohydrate. We have found through our research that this style of diet is also effective for losing weight and improving health. If eating more bread, pasta and rice is your preference, then this is the approach for you.

All of these dietary patterns, including the CSIRO Total Wellbeing Diet, share many similarities, such as:
- a high intake of vegetables
- recommendations for high-fibre and less-refined grain foods

- inclusion of low-fat dairy foods, and
- inclusion of lean meat, fish and poultry.

The eating plans differ only in the proportions of foods they recommend, but the CSIRO Total Wellbeing Diet is the only one of these plans that was designed specifically for weight-loss.

Our studies, and those of overseas researchers, have shown that a higher-protein, low-fat diet helps:

- preserve muscle during weight-loss
- enhance loss of fat
- improve vitamin B12 and iron status, and
- lower triglyceride levels in the blood.

In our studies, those people on a higher-protein diet lost the same amount of weight as those on a higher-carbohydrate diet, since the two diets offered an equal amount of kilojoules and the same amount of fat. However, body composition (that is, the ratio of fat to muscle) showed greater improvement among those people on the higher-protein diet. When the participants in other studies were allowed to eat until they were no longer hungry, those on the higher-protein diet lost more weight than those on the higher-carbohydrate diet, even after more than a year.

The reduction in hunger and the beneficial effect on muscle provided by the higher-protein diet is mostly related to its protein content, while the reduced triglyceride levels and enhanced fat-loss seem to be related to its lower amounts of carbohydrate. The diet is healthy because its protein comes from lean red meat, fish, chicken and low-fat dairy products, all of which provide good nutrition. A high-protein diet in which the protein comes from protein powders and supplements is unlikely to be healthy, unless the supplements are fortified with vitamins and minerals.

Do all protein sources have the same effect on reducing hunger? The answer is: most probably yes. Our studies at CSIRO have shown that animal and vegetable proteins seem to help reduce hunger for up to 4 hours after a meal, so that you don't feel the need for so many snacks.

What has changed since *Book One*?

The recommended requirements for vitamins and minerals have been revised by the National Health and Medical Research Council (NHMRC). As always, the scientists at CSIRO assisted in reviewing these requirements. The major changes recommended by this review were an increase in calcium and folate intake. The CSIRO Total Wellbeing Diet given in *Book One* met the original requirements, but the revisions have meant that we now recommend one extra dairy unit each day in the basic plan, to ensure adequate calcium intake. The level of kilojoules is slightly higher, but this will make very little difference to your weight-loss. The increase in recommended folate intake simply means that the minimum daily 2½ cups vegetables are now even more important. We have also made other minor changes to the eating plan, mostly to make it easier to understand and use from day to day.

part one

the
CSIRO Total
Wellbeing
Diet

what is the CSIRO Total Wellbeing Diet?

The CSIRO Total Wellbeing Diet is an eating and exercise plan for achieving a healthy lifestyle. It involves a structured eating plan (see pages 8–9) designed for weight-loss and subsequent weight-maintenance (see pages 25–6), as well as an exercise component (see pages 41–73). We have carried out extensive clinical evaluations of the eating plan for its efficacy in weight-loss, improving body composition, and reducing a range of cardiovascular and type 2 diabetes risk factors. We also found that the Diet improves nutritional status, as well as markers of heart health.

The Diet is best suited to overweight or obese adults, particularly those who have symptoms of metabolic syndrome (see page 4) – notably elevated levels of triglycerides and glucose in the blood, high blood pressure, low HDL cholesterol, and increased waist circumference. The eating plan is nutritionally complete and centred around the core food groups. The Diet is higher in protein than most diets, and low in saturated fat; it also provides moderate amounts of carbohydrate. The Diet provides more than the Recommended Daily Intake of nutrients (see page 219).

the basic plan – nutrition, nutrition, nutrition

Recent scientific studies have shown that not all forms of weight-loss are associated with good health and a long life. For example, losing excess weight as muscle tissue is bad news. Including enough protein and vital nutrients in your diet, and exercising regularly, will ensure that you achieve healthy fat-loss while minimising muscle-loss. The basic plan of the Diet (see pages 8–9) provides 5700 kJ a day. These kilojoules come mainly from proteins (about 30 per cent) and from high-fibre and slow-release (low-GI) carbohydrates (about 40 per cent). But the plan contains so much more. We have ensured a healthy level of good fats, particularly omega-3 fatty acids, and more than adequate amounts of vitamins and minerals for good health. The CSIRO Total Wellbeing Diet is about choosing nutritious foods in the right amounts combined with an exercise plan. For those with higher kilojoule needs, for example men, there are several levels of the Diet offering more kilojoules than the basic plan. See page 6 for how much of each food type is recommended at each level.

Understanding metabolic syndrome

At least one in four Australians has metabolic syndrome, many without even knowing it. Also known as syndrome X or insulin resistance syndrome, it's generally characterised by excess fat around the tummy, high blood pressure, high insulin levels, high blood glucose levels, high blood triglyceride levels and low blood levels of HDL or 'good' cholesterol. People with metabolic syndrome are at greater risk of developing heart disease and type 2 diabetes. However, if you are predisposed to metabolic syndrome, you can prevent its development by losing weight (as little as 3–4 kilograms will make a difference), eating healthily and exercising.

For a clinical diagnosis of metabolic syndrome, you are likely to have three or more of the following symptoms.

SYMPTOMS OF METABOLIC SYNDROME

symptom	women	men
waist circumference	greater than 88 cm	greater than 102 cm
triglycerides	greater than 1.7 mmol/L	greater than 1.7 mmol/L
blood pressure	greater than 130/85	greater than 130/85
HDL cholesterol	less than 1.3 mmol/L	less than 1.0 mmol/L
fasting glucose	greater than 6.1 mmol/L	greater than 6.1 mmol/L

Other characteristics of metabolic syndrome are sometimes used in diagnosis, for example a high blood insulin level. Whether you have metabolic syndrome or not, you can improve your health by losing a few excess kilos on the CSIRO Total Wellbeing Diet.

the main food types in the CSIRO Total Wellbeing Diet

The major protein sources for the Diet are:

- low-fat dairy products – 3 units a day

- lean protein foods – 2 units a day for dinner, up to 1 unit a day for lunch

The major carbohydrate sources are:

- wholegrain or fibre-enriched bread and cereals – 3 units a day

- fruit – 2 units a day

- vegetables – at least 2½ units a day

Major healthy fat sources are:

- oils, soft margarines, nuts, seeds – 3 units a day

Just one day (Level 1 plan)

Here's a snapshot of how any day on the CSIRO Total Wellbeing Diet might look.

Breakfast

40 g high-fibre cereal (e.g. Fibre Plus) with
250 ml low-fat milk and 150 g fruit
Breakfast = 1 unit cereal (see page 8),
1 unit dairy, 1 unit fruit

Lunch

2 slices wholegrain bread with 1 teaspoon margarine,
up to 100 g chicken, fish, pork, lamb, beef, or 2 eggs,
and ½ cup salad vegetables
Lunch = 1 unit protein, 2 units bread,
½ unit vegetables, 1 unit fats

Dinner

200 g (raw weight) beef, lamb, pork, chicken or fish
cooked in 2 teaspoons oil, with at least 2 cups
vegetables (from free list, see page 9)
150 g fruit with 200 g low-fat dairy dessert
Dinner = 2 units protein, 1 unit dairy, 1 unit fruit,
2 units vegetables, 2 units fats

Snack options

tea or coffee with low-fat milk
200 g low-fat yoghurt
Snack = 1 unit dairy

DAILY UNIT BREAKDOWN

3 units protein	red meat contains protein, well-absorbed iron, zinc, vitamin B12; fish contains protein, omega-3 fatty acids; chicken contains protein, zinc
1 unit cereal, 2 units bread	contains fibre, slow-release carbohydrate, B vitamins, magnesium
3 units dairy	contains calcium, protein, vitamin B12, zinc
2½ units vegetables, 2 units fruit	contains folate, vitamins A, B6 and C, fibre, magnesium, antioxidants
3 units fats	oils and margarines contain vitamin E; margarine also contains vitamins A and D

DAILY UNITS OF EACH FOOD TYPE

food type	amount each day (Level 1 plan)
low-fat dairy	3 units
lean protein	3 units (dinner 2, lunch 1)
high-fibre cereal/bread	3 units
healthy fats	3 units
vegetables/salad	at least 2½ units
fruit	2 units
Indulgences	2 units a week

energy needs and the CSIRO Total Wellbeing Diet

If you find you are getting too hungry on the basic plan, you are losing weight too quickly, or you are very active and have high energy needs, try moving to a higher level of the Diet. The table below gives the number of units of each food type allowed at each level. As a rule, women will lose weight on Level 1 or 2, while men will lose weight comfortably on Level 3 or 4.

ALLOWED FOODS ON LEVELS 1–4 OF THE CSIRO TOTAL WELLBEING DIET

level	1	2	3	4
daily energy intake (kJ)	5700	6200	7000	8000
dinner lean protein (units/day)	2	2	2.5	3
lunch lean protein (units/day)	up to 1	up to 1	up to 1	up to 1
wholegrain bread (units/day)	2	2	2	2
high-fibre cereal (units/day)	1	1	1¼	1¼
fruit (units/day)	2	2	2	3
low-fat dairy (units/day)	3	3	3	3
vegetables from free list (units/day)	2	2	2	2
salad (units/day)	½	½	½	½
fats and oils (units/day)	3	3	3	4
indulgence foods* (units/week)	2	9	9	9

* Includes alcoholic drinks or foods up to 450 kJ per unit, for example, 150 ml wine or 20 g chocolate

'No-one is overweight or needs to lose weight in our family of four, and we all lead relatively healthy lives, but I bought your book because of the menu planning, which includes all the food groups needed (as I was sure we were missing some). It's a fantastic fuss-free and informative guide. Well done! I'm a big fan of the no-fad stuff.'
– *Karina*

'I've gone from 69 kilos to 59 kilos (I'm only 158 cm tall) and my blood pressure has gone from borderline to 130 over 70. My cholesterol is 4.5. I've got into the black leather skirt I bought in 1990, and I've never had so many compliments! My husband was a bit resistant, being Italian and fond of his pasta, but he's lost 10 kilos too.'
– *Dianne*

'Before we started on the eating plan (which is what I prefer to call it, because it has just altered our eating habits), my husband weighed 132 kilos and his blood pressure was 180 over 110. He was a walking time bomb! Our doctor told him he could either lose weight or go on medication. After 11 weeks on the plan he has lost 16 kilos and his blood pressure is down to 110 over 80. His doctor is much happier and so are we. I've lost about 6 kilos, and have not felt this good in a long time.

'It's a plan that's affordable for an average working family and, as a working mum, I find the recipes easy to prepare, very tasty, and I can plan my shopping list for the week.'
– *Susie*

the CSIRO Total Wellbeing Diet

your daily food allowance

1 LEAN PROTEIN FOODS

– 2 units a day for dinner

1 unit is equal to 100 g raw weight of protein food. Eat 2 units lean red meat (beef, lamb or veal) for dinner 4 times a week. We recommend 2 units fish for dinner twice a week and 2 units fat-trimmed, skinless chicken or pork for dinner once a week.

2 LEAN PROTEIN FOODS

– up to 1 unit a day for lunch

Eat up to 100 g (raw weight) of any lean protein source (tinned or fresh fish or seafood, chicken, turkey, pork, ham, beef, lamb or 2 eggs) each day for lunch.

3 WHOLEGRAIN BREAD

– 2 units a day

1 unit is equal to one 35 g slice. You can replace one unit each day with any of the following:

- 1 slice fruit loaf
- 2 crispbread, such as Ryvita
- 1 medium potato (about 150 g)
- ⅓ cup of cooked rice or noodles
- ½ cup cooked pasta
- ⅓ cup baked beans, or cooked lentils, kidney beans or other legumes

4 HIGH-FIBRE CEREAL

– 1 unit a day

1 unit is equal to:

- 40 g any high-fibre breakfast cereal (e.g. Sultana Bran, Fibre Plus)
- 1 Weet-Bix plus ½ cup All-Bran
- 40 g rolled oats
- 1 slice wholegrain toast

5 DAIRY

– 3 units a day

1 unit is equal to:

- 250 ml low-fat milk
- 200 g low-fat or diet yoghurt
- 200 g low-fat custard or dairy dessert
- 25 g cheddar cheese or other full-fat cheese
- 50 g reduced-fat cheese (less than 10 per cent fat)

6 FRUIT

– 2 units a day

1 unit is equal to 150 g fresh or tinned, unsweetened fruit, 150 ml unsweetened fruit juice, or 30 g dried fruit.

basic plan

7 VEGETABLES
  – at least 2½ units a day from free list

1 unit is equal to 1 cup cooked vegetables. See free list opposite for vegetables you can eat. We recommend ½ unit salad and 2 cups cooked vegetables each day.

8 FATS AND OILS
  – 3 units added oils or fats a day

1 unit is equal to 1 teaspoon any liquid oil such as canola, olive or sunflower oil. 3 units oil is equal to:

- 3 teaspoons soft (trans-fat-free) margarine
- 6 teaspoons light margarine
- 3 teaspoons curry paste in canola oil
- 60 g avocado
- 20 g nuts or seeds

9 INDULGENCE FOODS
  – 2 units a week

1 unit is equal to any food or drink providing approximately 450 kJ, such as 150 ml wine or 20 g chocolate.

The free list: anytime foods and drinks

These foods contain minimal kilojoules, so eat them freely to spice up your meals.

vegetables artichokes, asparagus, bean sprouts, beetroot, bok choy, broccoli, Brussels sprouts, cabbage, capsicum, carrots, cauliflower, celery, chilli, chives, choko, corn, cucumber, eggplant, fennel, green beans, lettuce, marrow, mushrooms, onion, parsnips, peas, pumpkin, radishes, rhubarb, silver beet, spinach, swedes, tomatoes, turnip, zucchini

drinks Bonox, Bovril, cocoa, coffee, diet cordial, diet soft drinks, herbal tea, tea, unflavoured mineral water, water

condiments artificial sweeteners, barbecue sauce, chilli sauce, clear soup, curry powder, diet jelly, diet topping, fish sauce, garlic, ginger, herbs, hoisin sauce, horseradish, lemon, mint sauce, mustard, oil-free salad dressing or mayonnaise, parsley, pickles, soy sauce, spices, stock cubes, tomato paste, tomato sauce, Vegemite, verjuice, vinegar, wasabi

Note: It is acceptable to use small amounts of cornflour, custard powder or sugar to thicken or sweeten dishes. 1 level teaspoon cornflour, custard powder or sugar has 40–60 kJ. This is low enough not to worry about if you use them only occasionally. Always use salt sparingly.

salt and the CSIRO Total Wellbeing Diet by Jennifer Keogh

does salt matter when you're losing weight?

There's a well known connection between a high salt intake and high blood pressure. Cutting down on salt can reduce blood pressure, both in people with high blood pressure and those with normal blood pressure. Studies have also shown that people who lose weight on a diet low in salt have reduced risk of high blood pressure in the long term. When weight-loss and reduced salt intake are combined in older people, there is a dramatic reduction in the risk of high blood pressure and the need for medication. In our own studies we have seen that although blood pressure is reduced by weight-loss, it remains sensitive to salt intake.

how much salt should you have?

In its new recommendations, the National Health and Medical Research Council advises that 460–920 mg a day for adults is an adequate sodium intake and that intake should not go above 2300 mg sodium per day, which is the equivalent of approximately 6 g common table salt a day. This is a much lower amount than most Australians consume in their diet — estimates of intake range from 8 to 10 g salt per day. Salt occurs naturally in food, and there is rarely any need to add extra salt. While many people avoid adding salt in cooking and to salty foods, salt is included as an ingredient in many common foods such as bread and breakfast cereal, and is used as a preserving agent in many traditional foods. More than 75 per cent of our salt intake comes from processed foods.

is your salt intake relevant?

It is estimated that up to 50 per cent of the population will have developed high blood pressure by the time they retire. The best way to prevent this is through changes to your lifestyle: reducing your salt intake, losing weight and undertaking regular exercise. It's wise to have your blood pressure checked regularly by your GP, especially if you have a family history of high blood pressure, heart disease or stroke.

is there a low-salt version of the CSIRO Total Wellbeing Diet?

The CSIRO Total Wellbeing Diet minimises salt as much as possible, but since you are free to choose certain foods, your salt intake could go up without you really realising it. Try to minimise your use of processed meats for lunches, or make them special or occasional foods. Fresh (unprocessed) foods are naturally low in salt. See opposite for some suggestions for lower-salt meals.

common high-salt foods

Some foods are by their nature high in salt, for example, cheese and cured meats such as ham. Replace these foods with low-salt alternatives, such as milk or yoghurt instead of cheese, and roast cold meat, chicken or turkey instead of ham. Many brands of processed breakfast cereal and bread are also relatively high in salt. Good low-salt options are oats, either as porridge or in muesli, or low-salt cereal brands. Reduced-salt bread is available from some specialist bakers.

LOW-SALT OPTIONS FOR THE CSIRO TOTAL WELLBEING DIET

breakfast	lunch	dinner
• low-salt breakfast cereal, e.g. oats or oat-based cereals • yoghurt or fruit from your dairy and fruit allowances	• 100 g roast meat – chicken, turkey or beef • 2 eggs • 100 g tuna tinned in water • 100 g salmon tinned in water	• 200 g fish with vegetables (see below) • 200 g red meat – beef, veal or lamb • 200 g poultry – chicken or turkey • vegetables (fresh or frozen) or salad with vinegar or lemon juice • pasta, potato or rice, if included, are also low in salt

shopping for low-salt foods

To find the salt content of a product, look at the sodium content per 100 g on the food label. If the food contains 120 mg sodium per 100 g or less, then it is low in salt. For more information on food labels, see pages 22–23.

SALT CONTENT OF SOME LOW-SALT FOODS

food	mg sodium per serve	mg sodium per 100 g
instant oats	1.2 mg per 40 g	3 mg
rice cakes	0.4 mg per 2 cakes	2 mg
low-fat yoghurt	114 per 200 g tub	57 mg

your weight – take a reality check

We all know that weight can be a very sensitive issue for some people. In the 2001 National Health Survey, 6 per cent of men and 10 per cent of women would not disclose their height and weight. Most adults surveyed (64 per cent of men and 58 per cent of women), however, were reasonably happy with their weight, although 30 per cent of men and 38 per cent of women thought they were overweight. But we know that up to 66 per cent of adults are overweight or obese, so it seems that many of us don't know it or don't want to believe it!

The men surveyed seemed to be less concerned about their weight, and more men than women felt that their weight was acceptable when they were actually overweight. While 30 per cent of men thought they were overweight, in fact 58 per cent were overweight or obese. Women, on the other hand, had a better idea of their own weight; 42 per cent believed they had a weight problem, while 38 per cent actually did.

Men and women aged 45–74 years had the highest rate of obesity, while 68 per cent of men and 59 per cent of women aged 55–64 years carried excess weight. On the other side of the coin, 13 per cent of women aged 18–24 years were classified as being underweight.

Comparisons of these results with those from previous surveys show that Australians are getting fatter very quickly. In 1989–90 the proportion of men classified as overweight or obese was 46 per cent, by 1995 this had risen to 52 per cent, and in 2001 it was 58 per cent, an overall increase of 26 per cent in 11 years. The number of overweight or obese women increased even more during this time period, from 32 per cent in 1989–90 to 37 per cent in 1995 and 42 per cent in 2001.

body mass index (BMI)

A simple way to determine whether you are overweight and how much weight you need to lose is to calculate your Body Mass Index (BMI). In combination with your waist circumference, it can indicate your risk of type 2 diabetes, hypertension and heart disease.

BMI is a simple calculation of body fat. It's not perfect, but it's quick and easy. All you need to know is your weight (in kilograms or pounds) and your height (in metres or inches). Then you can calculate your BMI using one the following formulas:

BMI = weight in kilograms/(height in metres)^2
(i.e. your weight in kilograms divided by the square of your height in metres)

BMI = [weight in pounds/(height in inches)^2] x 703
(i.e. your weight in kilograms divided by the square of your height in inches, all multiplied by 703)

example
Arthur weighs 110 kg and is 1.88 m (188 cm) tall. His BMI would therefore be:

110 divided by 1.88 squared: $110/(1.88)^2 = 31.1$

By consulting the table below, we can see that Arthur is obese.

example
Joanne weighs 180 lb and is 5 feet 7 inches tall. Her height in inches would be $(5 \times 12) + 7 = 67$. Her BMI would therefore be:

180 divided by 67 squared, all multiplied by 703:
$[180/(67)^2] \times 703 = 28.2$

The table below shows us that Joanne is therefore overweight but not quite obese.

If you'd prefer to have a computer work out your BMI for you, try the BMI calculator on the Federal Government's healthy weight website, www.healthyactive.gov.au/internet/healthyactive/Publishing.nsf/Content/your-bmi.

what your BMI tells you

BMI	body condition
less than 18.5	underweight
18.5–24.9	normal
25.0–29.9	overweight
greater than 29.9	obese

Note: The BMI has the following limitations.
- It can overestimate body fat in athletes and people with a muscular build.
- It can underestimate body fat in older people and others who have lost muscle mass.
- The cut-offs are not applicable to all ethnic groups. For example, in people of Asian ancestry, excess fat may be present at lower BMI values.

waist circumference

Your waist circumference can be used in conjunction with your BMI to assess how much your excess body fat is putting your health at risk. If your BMI tells you that you are overweight and your waist circumference is greater than 102 cm for men or 88 cm for women, you are at greater risk of type 2 diabetes, hypertension and heart disease. Consult the following table for more information.

BMI, WAIST CIRCUMFERENCE AND ASSOCIATED DISEASE RISKS*

body condition	BMI	waist circumference less than 102 cm (men)/ 88 cm (women)	waist circumference greater than 102 cm (men)/ 88 cm (women)
underweight	less than 18.5	–	–
normal	18.5–24.9	–	increased
overweight	25.0–29.9	increased	high
obese	30.0–34.9	high	very high
	35.0–39.9	very high	very high
extremely obese	greater than 39.9	extremely high	extremely high

* Disease risk for type 2 diabetes, hypertension and heart disease.

healthy weight ranges

If you'd rather not calculate your BMI, here is a guide to healthy weight ranges. Suggested weights for men will tend to be at the upper end of the range and for women at the middle to lower end. Weight tables do not take into account your amount of muscle or fat, so this table is only a rough guide. You should not aim simply to lose weight until you are within the suggested range, but rather to eat better and exercise more. Even a small weight-loss, if permanent, will improve your health.

height		weight	
centimetres	feet and inches	kilograms	stones and pounds
142	4'8"	40–50	6 st 4 lb – 7 st 12 lb
145	4'9"	42–52	6 st 8 lb – 8 st 3 lb
147	4'10"	44–55	6 st 13 lb – 8 st 9 lb
150	4'11"	45–56	7 st 1 lb – 8 st 12 lb
152	5'0"	46–58	7 st 4 lb – 9 st 2 lb
155	5'1"	48–60	7 st 8 lb – 9 st 7 lb
157	5'2"	50–62	7 st 12 lb – 9 st 11 lb
160	5'3"	51–64	8 st 0 lb – 10 st 1 lb
163	5'4"	53–66	8 st 5 lb – 10 st 6 lb
165	5'5"	55–68	8 st 9 lb – 10 st 10 lb
168	5'6"	56–71	8 st 11 lb – 11 st 3 lb
170	5'7"	58–72	9 st 2 lb – 11 st 5 lb
173	5'8"	60–75	9 st 6 lb – 11 st 12 lb
175	5'9"	62–77	9 st 11 lb – 12 st 2 lb
178	5'10"	63–79	9 st 13 lb – 12 st 7 lb
180	5'11"	65–81	10 st 4 lb – 12 st 11 lb
183	6'0"	68–85	10 st 10 lb – 13 st 6 lb
185	6'1"	69–86	10 st 13 lb – 13 st 8 lb
188	6'2"	71–88	11 st 3 lb – 13 st 13 lb
190	6'3"	72–90	11 st 7 lb – 14 st 4 lb

alcohol and wellbeing

For many people, drinking alcohol is a way of winding down at the end of a busy working day, and it's true that moderate amounts of alcohol can act as a relaxant. Many people have commented that the alcohol restrictions in the CSIRO Total Wellbeing Diet are difficult to maintain. But there are several reasons why it's important to keep your alcohol intake very low when you are trying to lose weight. First of all, alcohol is a significant source of kilojoules. 1 g of alcohol provides 27 kJ, which adds up to 414 kJ in a standard 150 ml glass of wine, 550 kJ in a 375 ml can of beer and even more in mixed drinks with added fruit juice or soft drinks. These high-kilojoule drinks do not satisfy our appetite at all, nor add any essential micronutrients to our diet. In addition, because alcohol stimulates the biochemical pathways involved in appetite control, too much alcohol also means you can end up overeating. Thirdly, alcohol can slow down fat metabolism, making it even harder to lose weight.

Moderate alcohol intake also has benefits. An intake of 2 standard drinks a day has been associated with reduced risk of coronary heart disease. This seems to be because alcohol increases the level of HDL ('good') cholesterol in the blood. Alcohol also seems to reduce the formation of blood clots.

You do not need to become a teetotaller to lose weight, nor should you take up drinking alcohol if you don't already. But what is a safe and sensible approach to losing weight on the CSIRO Total Wellbeing Diet if you really enjoy having a drink more often than once or twice a week? If you do not want to lose weight, a safe intake of alcohol is 2 standard drinks a day for women and 4 for men (see more information overleaf). (Remember, an average glass of wine is more like 1.5 standard drinks – see table overleaf.) If you are trying to lose weight on the Diet, however, an alcohol intake of 1 standard drink a day will slow your weight-loss only slightly. If this works for you, great, but if you find that it sabotages your eating pattern, try 3 standard drinks a week.

how much alcohol is healthy?

The National Health and Medical Research Council provides the following guidelines for healthy alcohol intake. But remember, if you want to lose weight on the CSIRO Total Wellbeing Diet, you will need to drink less than this. The guidelines are different for men and women.

Men should observe the following guidelines for healthy drinking:

- an average of no more than 4 standard drinks a day, and no more than 28 standard drinks a week
- no more than 6 standard drinks on any one day, and
- 1 or 2 alcohol-free days a week.

Women should observe the following guidelines for healthy drinking:

- an average of no more than 2 standard drinks a day, and no more than 14 standard drinks a week
- no more than 4 standard drinks on any one day
- 1 or 2 alcohol-free days a week.

Note: You should always drink at a moderate rate and spread the drinks over several hours. For example, men should drink no more than 2 drinks in the first hour and 1 per hour thereafter, while women should drink no more than 1 drink per hour. If you have a medical condition or symptoms such as abnormal blood fats, high blood pressure, heart disease, heart failure, liver disease, diabetes or obesity, you should discuss your alcohol consumption with your GP.

what is a standard drink?

In Australia, a standard drink contains 10 g alcohol, which is the equivalent of 12.5 ml pure alcohol. It does not indicate a standard volume, since different drinks can have widely different alcohol contents. By law, the label must indicate how many standard drinks are in that container. The table below will help a little, but always check the label.

STANDARD DRINKS AND KILOJOULE COUNTS

drink	type	amount	kilojoules	standard drinks
wine	white, non-sweet	150 ml glass	414	1.5
	white, medium sweet	150 ml glass	414	1.5
	white, sparkling	150 ml glass	407	1.5
	red, still	150 ml glass	425	2.0
	red, sparkling	150 ml glass	407	2.0
beer	bitter/draught	375 ml can	550	1.5
	reduced alcohol (1.15–3.5% alcohol)	375 ml can	393	0.8
	stout	375 ml can	855	2.0
spirits	non-sweet	60 ml	514	2.0
port	standard	60 ml	374	0.8
liqueur	cream-based, coffee-flavoured	60 ml	867	1.0
	other (greater than 30% alcohol)	60 ml	1084	2.0

'I bought the book 3 months ago. It is my BIBLE! I'm coming up to the end of my 12th week and I have lost 15 kilos. I've gone from a size 18–20 down to a size 16. I'm ecstatic over my weight-loss, and so is my husband. Thank you, CSIRO. I've convinced a lot of people it works.'
– *Margaret*

'I've had polycystic ovary syndrome (PCOS) for 6 years, and have been married for 4 of those years. I'd tried all the typical PCOS strategies, but to no avail. Early in October I went on the CSIRO Total Wellbeing Diet and I have to say, after only a couple of weeks I felt a million dollars: weight-loss, energy, no anxiety.

'That's fantastic enough, but the plot thickens. Three months went by. I wasn't following the Diet too strictly, but I was doing okay. I finished my 12 weeks fitter, lighter and healthier than I had been for years. I went on holidays to Ireland and put my fatigue down to the stress of the international flight and jetlag. But here I am, 9 weeks pregnant and fingers crossed everything will work out. There are no guarantees, but my husband and I are stunned, as we were looking into IVF and adoption. We can't believe how this has worked out. Yep, the Total Wellbeing Diet got me up the duff (with a bit of help from my husband!), and I thought I'd let you know that it really works. Thanks, you've changed my life for the better.'
– *Erin*

tips for eating out

Eating out is always tricky when you're on a diet, but there is no need to avoid going out altogether. Try to limit your meals out to once a week during the weight-loss phase of your diet. Once you have moved onto the maintenance plan (see pages 25–6), you can eat out more often. Here are some simple tips for eating out without falling off the wagon.

1 Take it easy with the alcohol

- Alcohol contains lots of kilojoules and may also add kilojoules by increasing the amount you eat (see page 17).
- Alternate your alcoholic drinks with mineral water or a diet soft drink.
- Don't allow top-ups of your alcoholic drinks. They make it too easy to lose track of how much you're drinking!

2 Watch the nibbles

- If you're going to a friend's house for dinner or having friends over, be careful with the nibbles – they can be kilojoule kryptonite!
- Use vegetables rather than biscuits for dipping. Sticks of carrot, celery and cucumber, or mushroom caps, snowpeas, parboiled cauliflower and broccoli, all look fabulously colourful and appetising. Dips such as carrot and coriander, hummus, tzatziki, eggplant or beetroot taste great and are light on kilojoules.
- Include fruit as nibbles. Cherries, strawberries and slices of melon are great alternatives to the deep-fried morsels often served.
- Try to avoid salty chips, and biscuits and pastries. If serving nuts, leave them in their shells so that you can't eat them as quickly.
- Eat slowly and savour the taste. Spend more time talking, listening and laughing.

3 Count your courses

- It's helpful not to be over-hungry when you go out to dinner. A good idea is to eat one of your dairy units, such as a tub of yoghurt, an hour or so before going out. That should take the edge off your hunger for a while.
- If you're having more than one course, try to choose a soup as an entrée – vegetable-based soups are best. Remember to ask the chef not to add cream.

- Dishes consisting mainly of protein foods, such as smoked salmon, carpaccio, or chicken or prawn dishes, can be a good option if the meat has not been battered and deep-fried.
- If there are no suitable mains, a safe bet is to choose 2 entrées instead of an entrée and a main.
- Avoid hoeing into the bread and butter.
- If there is a set menu, don't eat everything on your plate. Eat all of the protein-food component and the free list vegetables, but only half the mash or chips.
- Restaurants never seem to serve main meals with enough vegetables these days. Always ask for a side salad or steamed vegetables on the side. They will slow down your eating and fill you up as well.
- Desserts are always tricky. If you can resist, great! If not, it's best to share one.

Interpreting food labels

Food Standards Australia New Zealand (FSANZ) is responsible for ensuring our food is safe. In Australia and New Zealand, all packaged foods, with some minor exceptions, must carry a nutrition information panel. The exceptions include foods in very small packages – for example, herbs and spices – foods that are sold unpackaged, and foods made and packaged at the point of sale.

The panel must list the amount of energy, protein, fat, saturated fat, carbohydrate, sugars and sodium (that is, salt) that the food contains. If the manufacturer makes a nutrition claim on a food label, they must include a nutrition information panel on the same label, with information on the nutrient about which the claim is made.

The nutrition information panel must be presented in a standard way and must include:

1 the amount of each nutrient per serve, and

2 the amount of each nutrient per 100 g (or 100 ml if liquid).

To compare one product with another, always check the 'per 100 g' column, as that way you will be comparing the nutrition offered in the same amount of food. The serving size listed on the nutrition information panel is determined by the manufacturer and will vary from product to product – it won't necessarily be the same as the package size. The 'per serve' information is useful in estimating how much of a nutrient you are eating – provided that your serving size is the same as that on the label.

If you're watching your weight, the most important information you need to check on the label is the number of kilojoules. Second comes the nutritional value, which will vary from one food type to another. If you are looking at dairy products, the fat and saturated-fat content are very useful guides to the best choices – lower-fat and lower-saturated-fat options are healthier. But of course, if you choose full-fat versions, you can eat a smaller portion. When looking at breads, fat is not generally an issue; what you are looking for is whether it is wholegrain, high in fibre and/or low-GI. For breakfast cereals, check the fibre panel; higher-fibre cereals are generally better options. Some cereals that are higher in fat may contain nuts, which contain healthy fats. Don't let the fat content of these foods put you off, as they can be healthy choices in controlled amounts. For protein foods, fat content is a good guide – the lower the fat, the fewer the kilojoules.

Things start to get a bit more complex when you look at snack foods like biscuits; the fat content alone is not a reliable indicator of how healthy the product is. First check the kilojoule content and then check if the product has any nutritional benefit. Does it contain any fibre or added vitamins? If not, it's probably a food to eat only occasionally, as a treat.

This might all sound a bit too complicated, but that's because there are many things to consider when choosing foods. One way to simplify things can be to choose foods that have the Heart Foundation's Tick. The Heart Foundation Tick Program has been developed to help us make healthier food choices quickly and simply. The Tick symbol tells us that a food is a healthier choice compared to similar foods.

Foods with the Tick have been independently tested to ensure they meet the Heart Foundation's strict standards for saturated fat, trans fat, kilojoules, salt and fibre. Tick foods must also have nutritional value. Only foods that meet the strict nutrition standards can receive the Tick, and there are no exceptions.

Once a food has earned the Tick, it is then subject to random testing. This means that at any time, without the food manufacturer being warned, the food is purchased from the supermarket by Tick and sent to an independent laboratory for testing, to ensure that it continues to meet Tick's standards. Foods that don't make the grade are out of the program.

The Tick appears on all sorts of foods, from lean red meat to fruit and vegetables, bread and even ice-cream. The Tick is particularly useful for determining the relative healthiness of products like convenience meals and snack foods.

For more information about the Heart Foundation and the Tick, go to www.heartfoundation.com.au/tick.

 CERT TM

the CSIRO Total Wellbeing Diet maintenance plan

Once you've reached your goal, you can begin to add foods to your eating plan so that you no longer lose weight, but maintain it. Some people will maintain their new weight at a higher kilojoule level than others, and it will require a little trial and error for you to work out which level is best for you. You will soon work out exactly how much you can eat to maintain your new low weight.

To maintain your weight, you can stay on the structured diet program but simply add more kilojoules from the foods you enjoy. Listen to your body, experiment, and slowly add new foods to your daily menus in 500 kJ 'blocks' (see the table overleaf for ideas). It's still extremely important to stick with the basic structure of the eating plan, to ensure you eat enough of each food type and maintain your levels of nutrition. Here are some basic guidelines for staying on track.

1 Make sure you include a lean/low-fat protein food serve at each meal.

2 Always choose wholegrain breads and cereals.

3 If adding snacks, plan them and make sure you stay within your block allowance.

4 Eat regular meals and always have breakfast (or at least brunch on the weekend).

Adding 500 kJ 'blocks'

Add foods in 500 kJ blocks each day, until you find you are maintaining your target weight. This approach gives you the flexibility to choose the same or different foods each day. If you're eating out, you can 'save' three of your 500 kJ blocks and enjoy a big night out. Here's how to add the blocks.

ADDING 500 kJ BLOCKS ON THE MAINTENANCE PLAN

week 1	Add 1 x 500 kJ block to your basic plan each day
week 2	If you're still losing weight, add another food block of 500 kJ to your daily food allowance
week 3	If you're still losing weight, continue to add a 500 kJ food block to your food allowance each day until you maintain your weight

Of course, if you start gaining weight rather than maintaining it, do not add any foods the following week. If your weight-gain is more than 1 kg, drop back to the previous week's plan. Once you reach the stage where your weight is stable, that should remain your eating plan.

Keep moving

Don't neglect your exercise program once you have reached your target weight. There are many benefits to be gained from regular exercise, both in terms of your health and in managing your weight.

ADDING 500 KJ BLOCKS ON THE MAINTENANCE PLAN

food	500 kJ block
low-fat milk	250 ml
wholegrain bread	1 x 35 g slice
fresh fruit salad	300 g
dry-roasted, unsalted almonds	20 g
potato crisps cooked in canola oil	1 x 21 g packet
avocado	¼
baked potato	150 g
cooked pasta	⅔ cup
lean beef, lamb, pork, chicken or fish	100 g
canned beans	140 g
cheese	30 g
cheesecake	75 g
oil	3 teaspoons
ice-cream	70 g
milk chocolate	25 g
wine	150 ml glass
beer	375 ml can
spirits	60 ml

5 weeks on the maintenance plan

Here's a snapshot of how you might incorporate 500 kJ blocks gradually over 5 weeks.

week 1 maintenance	Choose any 1 block, e.g. 1 extra-thick slice of toast at breakfast
week 2 maintenance	Choose any 2 blocks, e.g. 1 extra-thick slice of toast at breakfast + nuts as a snack
week 3 maintenance	Choose any 3 blocks, e.g. 1 extra-thick of slice of toast at breakfast + nuts as a snack + 25 g chocolate
week 4 maintenance	Choose any 4 blocks, e.g. 1 extra-thick of slice of toast at breakfast + nuts as a snack + 25 g chocolate + 1 medium glass of wine
week 5 maintenance	Choose any 5 blocks, e.g. 1 extra-thick slice of toast at breakfast + nuts as a snack + 25 g chocolate + 1 medium glass of wine + 1 extra serve fruit

Note: Only continue to add blocks if you are still losing weight. As soon as your weight stabilises, *stop* adding blocks.

a diet for all ages

'I'm a 35-year-old mother of two, living in Dubbo. I've always had an interest in food and nutrition, and have a degree in nutrition – unfortunately that doesn't make you immune to putting on weight! My husband and I have been on the CSIRO Total Wellbeing Diet for 6 weeks now. I just wanted to say how great we have both found it. It's been one of the few diets that has worked, and the only diet my husband has been enthusiastic about, as he is getting real results (and he really enjoys fish and meat).

'I was 72.2 kilos when I started and am now slightly less than 68 kilos. My husband has lost 5 kilos. We've both found the Diet easy to follow. The recipes are delicious and the shopping lists very helpful. It's also great to be finally fitting into my old clothes, plus I feel healthy on the inside.'
– Renee

'I'm 45 years old. I commenced the eating plan 6 months ago, and in my first week I lost 3 kilos. This totally spun me out. I never thought I'd lose that much weight in one week! When I started the eating plan I was 74.3 kilos and now I'm 62.8 kilos, which I reached 2 months ago. I'm so proud, because I've kept the weight off and done it without group support! I exercise by walking every day (well, most days) for 40 minutes or so on the beach nearby.

'With your wonderful eating plan, if I fall off the wagon, I try to make it a healthy binge. But if I do happen to eat 'badly', I just think, next meal I'll get back on track. I'd never been a lover of red meat, but now I look forward to my red meat nights. I experiment and make some things up myself, and really enjoy eating now – but for the right reasons. I can't thank you enough.'
– Sharon

'I'm the home person in our family and have put us all on the healthy eating plan from the CSIRO. We love it! It's great to have a fridge full of vegies. It's equally great to walk out of the supermarket feeling like we've just spent a couple of hundred bucks on healthy food! The kids are getting right into it and, aside from the odd chocolate breakout, we're enjoying it as well. The weekly shopping list is a very handy tool, and I find that we are not doing any shopping between times, which is much better for budgeting.'
– Dave

'My husband and I are 73 and 77, and have been followers of the CSIRO Total Wellbeing Diet since 2003. There has been criticism regarding the amount of red meat consumed on this diet, but it is up to the individual to use the Diet as a guideline for good eating. We use the measurements allowable for the 7-day eating plan and are usually below the allowed amounts, as we find that the recommended accompaniments satisfy our hunger. In fact, following this diet we never feel hungry.
– Edna & Jim

'I really feel I should write to tell you I'm more than happy with my results from your diet. I am 17 years old and needed to get into shape for the summer – I just wanted to lose a few kilos. I've been on the CSIRO Total Wellbeing Diet for about three-and-a-half months now. I used to weigh 69–70 kilos, but now I weigh 55 kilos, and I'm very happy. My body mass index is perfect and I feel great. Although I've finished going through all the weeks eating exactly what was in the book, I now eat whatever I want but in moderation. I've remained this weight for a while now. This diet has set me up for life and I'm going to stick with eating healthily. Thank you so much.'
– Eleanor

your questions answered

tell me about the diet

• **What are the main characteristics of the CSIRO Total Wellbeing Diet?**

The CSIRO Total Wellbeing Diet is essentially a nutritionally balanced diet with a high level of lean protein foods to prevent hunger. Most of the protein is derived from lean red and white meat, fish and low-fat dairy foods. The Diet also contains adequate fibre from whole grains, fruit and vegetables. At the heart of the Diet is the principle of cutting down on kilojoules — without which weight loss cannot be achieved. Unlike many other diets, the CSIRO Total Wellbeing Diet has been tested in many clinical trials and is scientifically proven to work.

• **How similar is the CSIRO Total Wellbeing Diet to the Atkins diet?**

The CSIRO Total Wellbeing Diet is a protein-plus, low-fat, moderate-carbohydrate diet and is very different from the Atkins diet, which is very low in carbohydrate and very high in fat. The Total Wellbeing Diet includes a moderate amount of low-GI (slow-release) carbohydrates and abundant fruit and vegetables. It is nutritionally balanced, providing all necessary vitamins and minerals.

• **Is the CSIRO Total Wellbeing Diet easy to follow?**

You should find the Diet easy to follow and maintain. In this book we have included lots of new tasty recipes to try (see pages 101–213). To make it even simpler, we provide you not only with a basic eating plan (see pages 8–9), but also with menu plans (see pages 75–99) and shopping lists (see pages 220–4). Maintaining the daily checklist on page 214 will also help you stay on track.

• **Is the CSIRO Total Wellbeing Diet a low-fat diet?**

The Diet is low in fat, especially saturated fat. The basic plan provides about 5700 kJ in total each day. Less than 30 per cent of these kilojoules come from fat (about 30–40 g), and saturated fats account for only 6 per cent of total energy intake.

• **Will I get hungry?**

On our protein-plus diet you are less likely to get hungry. It has been scientifically proven that high-protein foods are more satisfying than high-fat or high-carbohydrate foods. Of course, we don't eat only because we are hungry – but when we are actively trying to lose weight, hunger can be a problem. Not only does our eating plan include a sustaining level of protein – from red meat, pork, chicken, fish, dairy foods and eggs – it also contains some good slow-release, low-GI carbohydrate foods, which can also curb hunger.

• Will I get bored with the meals?

We have designed the Diet to include a wide variety of foods, with plenty of menu plans (see pages 75–99) and food ideas. Of course there are some indulgence foods that don't feature – and these have been left out on purpose. However, if you need a treat, choose a mini version of whatever takes your fancy, savour it slowly and enjoy!

• Do I need to count calories every day?

You don't need to count a thing. We've done all the counting for you. However, you do need to keep track of the foods you eat each day. Copy the checklist on page 214 (or download it from www.csiro.au/twd) and keep it handy.

• Is the Diet flexible enough for me to eat out?

Eating out is okay as long as you follow our guidelines (see pages 21–2). It is often quite easy to eat higher-protein meals when dining out, since most main meals tend to be protein-based dishes.

• How long should I be on the Diet?

We don't specify a duration for the Diet, since everyone will need to lose different amounts of weight, and will lose weight at different rates, but we do give sample menu plans for a period of 12 weeks. The Diet provides balanced eating, so once you have lost weight you can eat more indulgence foods. It is helpful, however, to keep to the basic eating pattern.

• Will it help me keep the weight off?

Because the Diet is easy to follow and can help you control your hunger, it is more sustainable in the longer term. Once you have reached a weight you feel comfortable with, you can switch to the maintenance plan (see pages 25–6), which allows greater flexibility. But your weight will stay low only if you continue to exercise and take care with your food choices. Keep at it, and don't panic if you 'fall off the wagon' occasionally.

I'm not sure what foods I can eat

• Do I have to eat all of the protein portion in a meal? Won't this be too much saturated fat?

The protein-plus diet doesn't suit everyone. You might find that you are better suited to a high-carbohydrate diet. Participants in our studies ate 200 g (raw weight) lean protein food at evening meals and 100 g (raw weight) chicken or fish at lunch. If you want to follow the CSIRO Total Wellbeing Diet, it is essential that you eat these items daily. The Diet is low in fat, since the protein-food allowances are based on lean, fat-trimmed cuts, and our studies have shown that blood cholesterol levels drop in people on the Diet. Higher-protein meals help control appetite and prevent muscle-loss while dieting. If you wish to eat less meat at lunchtime, you can try other lean protein foods, such as eggs or soy protein foods.

- **Can I change the order of meals and fiddle around with the times I eat the allocated foods?**

Absolutely! As long as you eat the foods specified on pages 8–9 and include some protein at each meal, it's not critical to eat the foods in any given order. Remember that the menu plans are only examples of how to put together the recommended foods. You can also choose your own menu and recipes as long as you don't exceed the required amounts of food in the daily plan. So it's quite okay to save something from a main meal, such as fruit or a low-fat dairy item, to have as a between-meal snack, or to swap lunch with dinner. Whatever you decide, remember that it's easiest to stick to the Diet if you establish a routine with your eating pattern.

- **If I follow the menu plans, I end up with lots of leftovers. What can I do?**

The main reason most menu plans have different meals for each day is to illustrate that there is scope for plenty of variety and flexibility. This does not mean, however, that you must have different meals every day. As all the recipes are designed for 4 people, the best solution when cooking for 1 or 2 is to halve the recipe amount or freeze any leftovers for later use. It is perfectly reasonable to have the same breakfast and lunch every day if you find that easier!

- **Why are vegetables on the free list but not fruit? Can I have more vegetables if I want to?**

The Diet has been created to provide a particular ratio of protein, fat and carbohydrate. Within this ratio, fruits and vegetables play an important part in providing essential nutrients and fibre. Vegetables are on the free list (see page 9) because they are lower in kilojoules than fruits. Fruits are generally limited on most diet plans because of the natural sugars they contain. The specified 2½ cups (about 375 g) vegetables a day is a benchmark. Feel free to eat more vegetables from the free list, but most people find eating even 2½ cups a day a challenge!

- **What is the difference between wholegrain and wholemeal bread, and does it matter?**

Wholegrain bread contains all the components of the grain – the bran, germ and endosperm. The grains may be whole, cracked or milled. In wholemeal bread, the whole grains have been milled to a finer texture to become wholemeal. Wholemeal bread therefore contains all the components of the grain, and so wholemeal foods are also wholegrain. It doesn't matter so much whether you have wholegrain rather than wholemeal bread, and vice versa; what is important is that the bread you choose is high in fibre. Australian food regulations state that a food must contain 3 g fibre per serve to be considered high-fibre. Always check the nutrition information on the packet to make sure you buy high-fibre bread. In our menu plans (see pages 75–99) and in our lunchbox ideas (see pages 103–113) we list different types of bread, but this is only to provide variety and taste rather than prescribing one type of bread for the entire dietary plan.

- **Is low-fat milk different from skim milk?**

Reduced- or low-fat milk contains 1–2 per cent fat, whereas skim or non-fat milk contains less than 0.16 per cent fat. In the Diet, 1 unit dairy is equal to 250 ml low-fat milk. You need to eat 3 dairy units a day on the basic plan (see pages 8–9).

- **Are lentils and beans considered protein or carbohydrate?**

They are a mixture of both. Lentils and butter beans are higher in protein than most vegetables, which mainly supply carbohydrate. However, lentils and beans also contain carbohydrate, and are not as high in protein as meat, fish, chicken or dairy foods. In the CSIRO Total Wellbeing Diet, you can eat chickpeas, beans or lentils instead of bread: 1 x 35 g slice bread = ½ cup cooked chickpeas, beans or lentils.

- **Can I eat sardines instead of tuna or salmon?**

You can eat 100 g lean protein (fish, chicken, pork, ham, lamb or turkey) for lunch each day, so sardines are perfectly acceptable, and are a fantastic source of omega-3 fatty acids and calcium. If the sardines are packed in oil, count this as part of your fat intake, unless you drain them.

- **Can I eat eggs?**

As eggs are basically a protein source, you can eat them instead of other protein foods. Substitute 1 egg for 50 g lean meat, chicken, turkey, pork, ham or fish.

- **How much sugar or honey can I have? Can I have artificial sweeteners?**

Although sugar is generally not included in the Diet, 1–2 teaspoons a day is fine. Artificial sweeteners will not affect your kilojoule intake, so they will not ruin your diet.

- **What can I eat for snacks?**

Here are some alternative morning- and afternoon-tea ideas: from your dairy allowance a skim-milk cappuccino or latte, or a 200 g low-fat yoghurt, custard or Frûche; or from your fruit allowance 1 piece (150 g) fruit. Tea or coffee with a dash of milk is fine. A low-kilojoule soup as part of your vegetable allowance is a great option as well.

- **How much vegetable or tomato juice can I have?**

You could substitute a quantity of unsweetened vegetable juice for vegetables, but remember that juicing may extract fibre, which is an important reason for eating vegetables. Up to 2 cups vegetable juice a day is fine to include in addition to or as part of your daily vegetable intake.

I want to include the family

- **Will I be able to feed my whole family with the suggested meals?**

Yes, you will. The recipes fit easily into family meal plans. However, members of the family who do not need to lose weight may need to include extra carbohydrate foods in their meals, such as bread, pasta, rice or potatoes.

- **Is the Diet applicable to men?**

It can be a healthy weight-loss approach for men. Because men tend to be taller and heavier than women, we would suggest Levels 2, 3 or 4 of the Diet. Many men have used the Diet very successfully.

- **Is the Diet suitable for children and teenagers?**

The diet is adequate for overweight children and teenagers from a nutritional perspective. However, the number of kilojoules will need to be adjusted for the age, size and activity level of the child, which is best done by a qualified dietitian. Because children are growing, excessive kilojoule restriction can affect their growth, so some care needs to be taken to ensure that their diet is not overly restrictive. We would recommend smaller weight-losses each week than for adults, unless the child is very overweight. Sometimes even keeping their weight stable as they grow will result in fat-loss. If the whole family is eating meals based on the CSIRO Total Wellbeing Diet, this will provide good nutrition for everyone. Extra snacks (mostly fruit and low-fat dairy snacks) may be necessary for some overweight children. We recommend you consult your GP and seek a referral to a dietitian, who will keep an eye on your child's weight and growth.

I have special dietary requirements

- **Is there a diet for vegetarians?**

We have not investigated whether a high-protein vegetarian diet is as effective as a high-animal-protein diet, but we do know that vegetable protein confers a similar benefit in reducing hunger. You may want to consult your GP or dietitian to modify the Diet for your needs. If you wish to substitute non-meat protein, we would suggest eating 200 g tofu or 260 g cooked chickpeas, beans or lentils instead of 200 g meat, fish or chicken.

- **I don't usually eat much red meat. Is there something else I can eat for lunch?**

It is not necessary to eat red meat at lunchtime. You can choose instead to eat 2 eggs or 100 g fish or chicken.

- **Can I use the Diet while I'm pregnant or breastfeeding?**

The CSIRO Total Wellbeing Diet is a safe eating plan, but if you have concerns while pregnant or breastfeeding, you should consult your GP or a dietitian regarding meal sizes and their nutritional content. The 3 units dairy recommended in the basic plan of the Diet (see pages 8–9) will provide adequate calcium intake for pregnant and breastfeeding women. The recommended daily intake of folate for pregnant and breastfeeding women is 500–600 µg. Good sources of folate include: leafy green vegetables, bananas, berries, apricots, melons, oranges, chickpeas, lentils, dried beans and peas, peanuts, almonds, sunflower seeds, wheat germ, wheat bran, breads, fortified breakfast cereals, liver and kidney. If you are planning a pregnancy, make sure you take a folate supplement. Depending on how often you are breastfeeding, your daily kilojoule requirements may increase by up to 3000. We suggest starting with Level 3 (7000 kJ a day) then see how you go. It's important to monitor your milk supply and ensure you drink plenty of fluids, get sufficient calcium, and take regular exercise.

- **I have diabetes. Is the Diet appropriate for me?**

If you have diabetes you should check with your GP, dietitian or specialist to make sure the Diet is appropriate for you.

- **What if I can't eat dairy foods?**

If you need to substitute soy products for dairy, use the same quantities of low-fat, high-calcium soy milk products as given for dairy foods.

- **Can I use the Diet if I am gluten-intolerant?**

We advise checking with your GP, nutritionist or specialist that the Diet is suitable for you. However, you should be able to use it by substituting equivalent quantities of similar foods, for example replace 1 x 35 g slice bread with ½ cup cooked beans, lentils or chickpeas or 35 g gluten-free bread.

- **I have irritable bowel syndrome and can't eat bran. How can I ensure adequate fibre intake?**

The recommended daily intake of dietary fibre is 30 g. The CSIRO Total Wellbeing Diet ensures adequate fibre intake through wholegrain foods, fruits and vegetables. People with irritable bowel syndrome can take supplements (such as psyllium) to help maintain adequate fibre intake, or products such as probiotics may be of assistance. Probiotics are foods containing live bacterial cultures, for example some yoghurts. You should always discuss your medical issues with your GP before embarking on any new dietary regime.

- **I am fructose-intolerant. Can I adapt the Diet?**

We do not deal with such specific medical concerns. We suggest you contact the Allergy and Environmental Sensitivity Support and Research Association Inc. (AESSRA), who can provide information on treatment, services and products: (03) 9888 1382. Food Standards Australia New Zealand (FSANZ) has also issued advice to fructose-intolerant people to avoid the new food ingredient tagatose.

I need shopping tips

- **How can I reduce my food bill?**

Try to shop for what is seasonally available, particularly with fruit and vegetables. Also buy less expensive cuts of meat. Cheaper lean mince is fine, as are cuts that need more cooking time, such as chuck steak for stews. These can be cooked in bulk on the weekend and frozen in batches. Choose less expensive fish varieties, as well as canned fish. To bring down the cost of lunches, replace one of the protein-food units with an extra dairy unit or 2 eggs. If that doesn't bring down costs enough, try making dinner with 100 g portions of red meat, chicken or fish along with 130 g beans or lentils (cooked weight) or 100 g tofu. Remember, the eating plans are a guide only, and can be varied as long as you choose alternatives from the same food groups.

- **Is there a version of the shopping lists with quantities on it?**

The amounts of food needed will depend on how many members of your household are on the Diet and how many of you are eating the suggested main meals. You need to photocopy these pages and then fill in the required quantities yourself, or download the lists with quantities from www.csiro.au/twd.

please explain the exercise component

• How does physical activity play a part in the CSIRO Total Wellbeing Diet?

Exercise is essential to any weight-loss program and to your general health and wellbeing. We provide a complete exercise program in this book (see pages 41–73).

• Do I need to exercise?

We appreciate that some people may find exercising difficult, especially if they are overweight. If this is you, be assured that as you lose weight it will become easier to exercise. However, it is important that you take a walk as briskly as possible for 30 minutes at least 3 times a week. Check out the CSIRO Exercise Plan on pages 41 73.

I'm worried about potential health problems

• Will the Diet be bad for my health?

Losing even a few kilograms can have a positive effect on your health. Our protein-plus diet has been tested for its impact on kidney, liver and bone health, and we have seen no adverse effects. If you have any pre-existing medical condition, such as diabetes, or if you are taking medication, check with your GP first, to ensure that the eating plan is right for you.

• Isn't there too much/too little food in the Diet?

Some people have told us that the daily amounts of food are too little or too much for them. If you find this is the case, remember that you can always swap your lunch and dinner if you prefer to eat less at night. Shift-workers could spread out the components of each meal through the day or night. As long as your total daily intake remains the same and you have the correct amount of each food type, it doesn't really matter when you eat it.

• I usually eat quite a high-carbohydrate diet. Can the CSIRO Total Wellbeing Diet lead to ketosis?

When fat is broken down in the body of people on a very low-carbohydrate diet, their liver cannot burn some of the end products, and these are converted into ketones, which the heart can use for energy. This process, known as ketosis, does not occur on the CSIRO Total Wellbeing Diet.

• Wouldn't I be setting myself up for heart disease if I ate this much red meat?

Two units of lean red meat for dinner 4 times a week, fish for dinner twice a week and chicken for dinner once a week are key elements of the CSIRO Total Wellbeing Diet. In fact, protein-rich foods will help control your blood fats, so don't be concerned that eating more protein will increase your cholesterol levels. Just remember to choose lean cuts of red meat and pork, remove skin from chicken and opt for low-fat dairy products.

- **Did I read correctly that the Diet lowers HDL cholesterol levels? Isn't this good cholesterol?**

The CSIRO Total Wellbeing Diet can result in a beneficial reduction in triglycerides and LDL (bad) cholesterol, and sustained weight-loss actually increases HDL (good) cholesterol. Regular exercise and a moderate alcohol intake are two factors that have also been shown to increase the level of HDL cholesterol.

- **Isn't margarine bad for you, as it contains trans fatty acids that clog our arteries? Why don't you promote flaxseed oil or olive oil, which provide wonderful health benefits?**

Trans fats are formed when oil is processed to make margarine, and they are also found in beef and dairy fat. The CSIRO Total Wellbeing Diet is low in fat: you will be eating only 3 teaspoons margarine (or 6 teaspoons light margarine) a day at the most, so your intake of trans fatty acids will be low. Additionally, the major Australian margarine manufacturers have removed trans fatty acids from many of their products. Some convenience foods and high-fat manufactured foods contain trans fatty acids. Olive oil and canola oil are suitable for use in cooking, whereas flaxseed oil, although it does contain healthy omega-3 fatty acids, is not suitable for cooking. Because the Diet contains significant quantities of fish, it provides sufficient amounts of long-chain omega-3 fatty acids, which means that plant sources of omega-3 fatty acids are not required.

is red meat a risk factor for colorectal cancer?

Higher-protein, red-meat diets are very effective for weight-loss, but some people have expressed concerns that a high intake of red meat increases the risk of colorectal (bowel) cancer. Is this really so?

The evidence that eating red meat, or any single food, is a risk for colorectal cancer is weak at best, compared to the proven negative effects of being overweight and inactive. The key risk factors are:

- age – the risk is highest in people over 50
- gender – women have a higher risk of colon cancer, men of rectal cancer
- family history – a family history of colorectal cancer increases your risk
- diabetes – the risk increases by 30–40 per cent in people with diabetes
- lifestyle – high alcohol intake, smoking, lack of exercise, high kilojoule intake and obesity all increase your risk.

Being overweight can increase the risk of colorectal cancer by 70 per cent – and by up to 340 per cent in women – while exercise can reduce it by 20–70 per cent. The biggest lifestyle risks by far are being overweight and lack of exercise.

Studies have shown that fresh red meat (beef and lamb) is not a significant risk factor for colorectal cancer. A high intake of *processed* meat – greater than 560 g a week – increases the risk slightly. However, people who eat lots of red meat but also eat lots of fish are not at any increased risk. Risk *is* increased by excessive alcohol consumption, in conjunction with low vitamin and mineral intake.

Lean red meat is a good source of a number of important, potentially anticarcinogenic vitamins and trace elements, including antioxidants such as zinc, selenium, carnosine and anserine. The lean red meat in the Diet provides appropriate levels of protein, iron, zinc and vitamin B12.

The CSIRO Total Wellbeing Diet recommends 800 g lean red meat a week, and at least 400 g fish a week. The Diet advises low alcohol intake and provides all the necessary vitamins and minerals each day. The calcium and vitamin D provided by the Diet may actually protect against cancer.

The risks are further reduced by high fibre intake. In fact, studies have shown that there is no risk associated with meat of any kind when combined with a high-fibre diet. The CSIRO Total Wellbeing Diet provides a fibre intake in excess of 28 g a day from fruits, vegetables and whole grains. The Diet also recommends increased physical activity, which further reduces the risk of colorectal cancer.

All the evidence suggests that the CSIRO Total Wellbeing Diet is a safe and effective dietary method for weight-loss and maintenance, particularly in obese or overweight people.

Testing for colorectal cancer

More than 15 500 cancer deaths each year are due to smoking, sun exposure, poor diet, alcohol, inadequate exercise or being overweight. Colorectal cancer is the most common cancer in Australia after non-melanoma skin cancer, and it is the second leading cause of cancer death after lung cancer. One in 20 Australians will develop colorectal cancer in their lifetime. It can be treated successfully if detected early, but at the moment this happens for fewer than 40 per cent of colorectal cancers.

The CSIRO, through the Preventative Health National Research Flagship, is working on a range of preventative and early detection projects for colorectal cancer. These include work on protective foods, finding new ways to detect the disease in its early stages, and motivating people to test themselves for the cancer using a simple home-based kit.

The federal government has allocated $43.4 million over three years for a National Bowel Cancer Screening Program, which is to be phased in over a number of years from mid-2006. Initially, screening will be offered to Australians turning 55 or 65, and to those who participated in the pilot program. However, if you are not in the targeted age group and would like to be screened, you should to talk to your GP or pharmacist.

change your life

'In February this year I was diagnosed with polycystic ovary syndrome (PCOS) and was devastated, given its potential impact on my plans to start a family. I was told that weight-loss would be beneficial in reducing the side effects of PCOS. I had dieted on and off for most of my life, and had always found it difficult to lose weight, but more importantly to maintain a healthy body weight once I had achieved weight-loss. I heard about the CSIRO Total Wellbeing Diet over a year ago. Given its benefits for women with symptoms of metabolic syndrome, I became hopeful that this diet could work for me. I've followed the program for 8 weeks and have lost 6 kilos. My target is to lose a further 5 kilos, and I'm convinced I can achieve this. The best thing about the Diet is that I don't get those bouts of hunger that I've experienced on other diets. I feel satisfied and healthy overall, and I know I'm doing all I can to manage my PCOS. The book has given me information on the effects of food, and has equipped me to make food choices suitable for me. Thank you for your work in developing this program. It has definitely made a difference to my life!'

'. . . Since I last wrote to you, as a result of my weight-loss I'm now expecting my first baby, due in two months!'
– Sarah

'I'd like to thank the CSIRO for the Total Wellbeing Diet ("eating plan", I call it). My father died of a sudden heart attack aged 61, and Mum has middle-age-onset [type 2] diabetes with a history of it in the family. Approaching 50, at 155 cm and 100 kilos, I'd been lucky to avoid any major health problems. I commented to a friend that I really, really needed to lose some weight, and she told me about your diet. I've lost more than 6 kilos, and centimetres off my waist, hips and upper arms. I walk several mornings a week and do a 10 km bike-ride on other days. I have more energy, more balance and even run (which I haven't been able to do for several years!). I have two young adult children and a husband – with a few individual variations, the whole family follows the eating plan. Thank you to all who took part in developing this eating plan. You've made a nearly 50-year-old so proud of herself.
– Mary

'I just wanted to let you know that I absolutely love the eating plan. I bought the book a few months ago and lost 5 kilos, which is exactly what I wanted! I'm one of those people who are physically demonstrating to all around them that the Diet does indeed work. I feel better and healthier than I ever have! I love the versatility of the Diet, and the basic set of rules.

'There's no magic answer, but your book is the closest thing I've found. It's sensible and I love it. I can follow the principles of it beyond the life of the book, too. I'm really happy with myself for the first time in a while. My greatest thanks. You've made a big difference in my life.'
– Lisa

'I'm 58 years old, and for me the CSIRO Total Wellbeing Diet has been an incredible experience. I'm thrilled to bits with it, and I recommend it to many people. Everywhere I go I just keep talking to people about it, whether I know them or not. For someone who was as obese as I was, this is the most remarkable diet I've ever tried. The support of friends and family has been great too.

'I started the CSIRO Total Wellbeing Diet a year ago. I've lost 25 kilos so far, and am aiming at losing another 25 kilos this year. I went out walking this morning, and even though it was quite warm, managed to walk more than 2 km.'
– Daphne

part two

the CSIRO exercise plan

by Dr Grant Brinkworth

the benefits of exercise

Remember, you are never too old to start exercising. The important health benefits of exercise are fairly immediate and can be achieved whatever your age, and regular physical exercise will keep you living longer and feeling younger. In fact, people who do not exercise are almost twice as likely to die from heart disease as those who participate in regular, moderate physical activity.

Combined with the CSIRO Total Wellbeing Diet's energy-reduced eating plan, participation in regular physical activity plays a key role not only in further improving your health and wellbeing but also in maintaining a stable body weight once you have lost those extra kilos. In fact, scientific evidence indicates that a combination of diet and exercise is the most effective approach for weight-loss. The great majority of successful weight-losers who maintain their reduced weight over a long period are those who have engaged in a regular exercise program. We can't emphasise enough the benefits of keeping active and exercising for long-term weight maintenance.

You must engage in adequate levels of physical activity if you are to achieve weight maintenance in the long term.

Current guidelines, based on scientific evidence, recommend participation in at least 150 minutes a week of moderate-intensity physical activity. This can have a positive impact on a number of health-related factors. It can:

- improve the health of your heart and lungs
- reduce your blood pressure and blood glucose levels
- reduce your blood cholesterol and triglyceride levels
- reduce your risk of a number of chronic diseases, including type 2 diabetes, heart disease, atherosclerosis, cancer, osteoporosis and arthritis, and
- improve your mood, confidence and sense of wellbeing.

But to get the most from your physical activity and ensure weight control, we recommend slightly higher levels of physical activity; scientific research suggests at least 200–300 minutes a week. We recommend 30–60 minutes of accumulated moderate-intensity physical activity (such as brisk walking) on most, and preferably all, days of the week. The simple fact is, the more exercise you can do, the greater the health benefits you will achieve and the easier it will be for you to lose weight or to maintain your new low weight.

The health benefits of regular exercise are greatest when you combine aerobic exercise with strength and flexibility training. Remember, you can also increase your fitness and burn extra kilojoules in your day-to-day activities – even vigorous housework and gardening count.

no time?

One of our biggest problems with doing sufficient physical activity is finding the time in our busy lives. We can make excuses all day about our lack of physical activity and the way everything in society has made it easier to be lazy, but it all comes down to how much we value our health and quality of life. The only real way you are going to improve your health is by investing time and effort in it. Put simply, if you have time to watch a television show or for any other appointment, then you have time to exercise. Don't let your health – or lack of it – stop you from enjoying the fun parts of life! The key is not to make exercise an optional activity or an inconvenience. Many people find it easy to participate in regular physical activity if they make it part of their essential daily routine, performed at the same time each day. So, to fit fitness into your life, choose exercise activities that suit your lifestyle and that can become a fun part of your daily routine.

incidental exercise

In addition to the planned exercise program outlined here, take advantage of any opportunity throughout the day to be physically active, whether this be at home, at work or during leisure periods. Remember, it all counts, and there are plenty of ways to incorporate exercise into your normal daily life. Take the stairs (instead of the lift or escalator) or keep walking while you're on the escalator, do some gardening, get off the bus two stops early and walk the rest of the way. Walk, run or cycle to work or the shops instead of taking the car. Go for a walk at lunchtime instead of reading a magazine. Organise a group of workmates, friends or family to walk with you so that you can keep each other on track. It will give you a great chance to catch up, and it will make exercising much more fun. The contribution of incidental exercise to your total energy expenditure is significant, and may be just as beneficial as your planned exercise program.

aerobic exercise

The core of your exercise program should be regular, moderate-to-vigorous aerobic exercise that will improve your cardiovascular fitness. This form of exercise also requires the greatest energy expenditure and so will have the biggest impact on weight-loss by burning that excess fat. The type of aerobic exercise you do – walking, jogging, cycling, swimming or rowing – is up to you. Just remember, if the exercise is fun and you enjoy it, you will have a better chance of sticking to it. However, walking and jogging are probably the easiest forms of exercise in terms of the equipment, and basic fitness and skills required; they also give you the best overall body workout, and have many known health benefits. Walking carries a low risk of musculoskeletal injury as well.

strength training

An important adjunct to your aerobic exercise program is regular strength training, which can really help you maintain muscle strength and endurance. By preserving muscle, you increase your metabolic rate, helping your body burn more kilojoules, even at rest, which will make weight-loss easier. Strength training can also help reshape your body by improving muscle tone, and has a beneficial effect on your blood sugar levels. Your increased muscle strength will also improve your ability to perform daily functional tasks, such as lifting shopping bags, walking up stairs or pruning the hedge. This in turn may help you to adopt a more active lifestyle, and so increase your likelihood of weight-loss success. And ladies, don't worry, you aren't going to bulk up like a body builder! In fact, strength training can give you a slimmer, more shapely figure.

You should aim to complete your strength-training workout at least twice a week, but you don't need to go to a gym; there are many simple exercises you can do in your home without expensive equipment, such as the resistance tube workout provided in this book.

before you start

Initial health assessment

We strongly advise you to consult your doctor before undertaking the CSIRO Exercise Plan or any other exercise program, particularly if you are over 50.

Preparation

When exercising, ensure you wear comfortable, flexible shoes and light, loose-fitting clothing. Try to find a walking route in your local area that will allow you to walk comfortably; avoid damaged streets, high traffic zones and poorly lit areas. Don't let the weather be your excuse not to go for a walk: shopping centres provide a temperature-controlled environment with a smooth walking surface.

To prevent injury you should always warm up before you exercise, and cool down afterwards.

Warm-up (5–10 minutes)

Warm up the muscles you will be using in your exercise session. This will make them more pliable and less prone to injury. Begin with a few minutes of low-intensity aerobic activity using the mode of exercise you are about to engage in, such as a light walk or jog. Even a gentle jog on the spot is a great way to warm up the large muscles in your legs. You should feel your body heat rise and your breathing rate start to increase. This should be followed by gentle stretching of the muscles you are going to be exercising (see pages 47–50 for suggested stretches).

Cool-down (5–10 minutes)

Every structured exercise session should conclude with a cool-down period, to help return your cardiovascular system to normal before you stop moving completely. This is best achieved by gradually slowing down your exercise pace during the last several minutes of your workout. Complete the cool-down by stretching (see pages 47–50); this may help prevent muscle stiffness and improve flexibility. Use the same type of activities and stretches for your warm-up and cool-down.

Training diary

A training diary (see pages 216–17) can be a valuable aid. By providing a prompt for exercising and supplying feedback on your progress, it helps you stay on track and focused on your goals, and allows you to figure out what works best for you. It should include a record of your exercise each day, as well as how you felt during and after the period of exercise. Also remember to write your goals down – keep them simple and be realistic but specific. Keep your diary visible, so that you are constantly reminded of what you are trying to achieve and how to get there.

Exercise rules

Don't forget to:

- get your doctor's advice before starting any exercise program
- start at a level that is comfortable for you
- stretch to warm up and cool down
- hold off moving to the next level until you are comfortable doing so
- keep a regular training diary to record and monitor your progress, and
- drink plenty of water before, during and after exercise, to remain adequately hydrated.

Don't miss an exercise session because you think you don't have the time. Remember, the time you spend exercising will significantly improve your quality of life in so many ways, and allow you time to relax, think and focus. But if you *do* miss an exercise session, whatever the reason, don't be too hard on yourself and don't give up. Stay motivated and remain focused on your goals and what you are trying to achieve. Exercise can have an impact on every aspect of your physical health, from the way you look to the way you feel. That is reason enough to keep going!

stretching exercises

- Only perform stretches after you have done a light warm-up (see page 46).
- Do not bounce, and always stretch only to the point of mild tension, without discomfort. If you overstretch you will cause damage. Back off if the stretch feels painful.
- Do not hold your breath during the stretches. Breathe slowly and naturally.
- Hold each stretch for 10–20 seconds and repeat 2–3 times.

LOWER-BODY STRETCHES

Calves

1 Lean against a wall with your forearms or palms.
2 Place the leg you want to stretch straight back behind you, with your heel firmly planted on the floor, your front leg bent and positioned about halfway between your back leg and the wall.
3 Starting with your back straight, gradually move your hips forward and bend the knee of your front leg until you feel a stretch in the calf muscle of your back leg. Keep your back heel flat, your toes pointing straight ahead and your hips and shoulders parallel to the wall.
4 Repeat on the other side.

Hamstrings

1   Sit on the floor with both legs straight out in front of you.
2   Bend your left leg and place your left foot beside your right knee.
3   Keeping your left leg relaxed, your back straight and your head facing forwards, slowly bend at the hips (not waist) towards your right foot, until you feel a stretch in your right leg.
4   Repeat on the other side.

Quadriceps

1   Lie on your side, with your knees together.
2   Contract your abdominal muscles and, keeping your lower leg straight, bend the top leg, grasping your foot behind you. If you can't reach your foot comfortably with your hand, wrap a towel or belt around it and grasp this with your hand.
3   Slowly pull your foot towards your buttock, while slowly pushing your pelvis forward until you feel a stretch in your upper thigh.
4   Repeat on the other side.

Inner thighs

1   Stand with your feet pointed out slightly and a little more than shoulder-width apart. If necessary, hold on to something (such as the back of a chair) for balance.
2   Keeping your right leg straight, bend the knee of your left leg, moving your hip towards your left knee and leaning to the left.
3   Repeat on the other side.

UPPER-BODY STRETCHES

Upper back

1. Stand with your feet hip-width apart and your knees slightly bent.
2. Interlock your fingers and turn your palms out.
3. Keeping your body upright, extend your arms out in front at shoulder height, until you feel a stretch between your shoulder blades.
4. Hold, relax and repeat.

Shoulders and back of upper arm

1. Stand upright with your feet shoulder-width apart.
2. Bring one arm straight across your chest towards your other shoulder.
3. Keeping your upper body stable, ease your elbow across your chest and towards the shoulder with your other arm.
4. Repeat on the other side.

Shoulders

1. Stand with your feet shoulder-width apart.
2. Interlock your fingers above your head, palms facing upwards.
3. Push your hands further above your head as you exhale. You should feel a stretch in your shoulders.
4. Hold, relax and repeat.

Chest

1 Stand tall, with your feet shoulder-width apart and your knees slightly bent.
2 With your arms behind you, interlock your fingers, palms facing outwards.
3 Stretch your arms back as far as possible, pulling back your shoulders and sticking out your chest. You should feel the stretch across your chest and in the front of your shoulders. Ensure that you do not bend forwards.
4 Hold, relax and repeat.

Triceps

1 Stand with your feet hip-width apart and your knees slightly bent.
2 Place one hand down the centre of your back, touching between your shoulder blades, fingers pointing downward. Ensure your shoulders are relaxed.
3 Use your other hand to grasp your elbow and pull down on it gently, aiming to push your fingers down your spine.
4 Repeat on the other side.

Sides

1 Stand tall, with your feet slightly wider than shoulder-width apart and your knees slightly bent.
2 Lift your left arm above your head, with your elbow bent and your hand over your head.
3 Bend slowly to your right at the waist, reaching your lifted arm over and across until you feel a stretch in your side. Do not lean forwards or backwards.
4 Hold, return to an upright position, then repeat on the other side.

diet and exercise – a winning combination

'I spent the first 30 years of my life around 44 kilos, could eat like a horse, never put on weight and loathed physical exercise. Between 30 and 40 I crept up to 50 kilos. Once I turned 40 I steadily got heavier, even though I started to exercise daily and was very conscious of what I ate. I am now 58 years old and, up until recently, was 66.5 kilos.

'I commenced the CSIRO Total Wellbeing Diet two months ago. I haven't really followed the set menus, but have used the recipes. My aim has been to follow the principles behind it, and I can tell you that it has worked a treat for me. I started out at 66.5 kilos, as I said, and, as I am only 160 cm tall, I was edging up from a size 14. I'm now 57.5 kilos and can fit into a size 10, which I haven't been able to do for nearly 20 years! My aim is to get down to 56 kilos and stabilise my weight there.

'What had happened over the years, I now realise, was that I ate less and less protein. I'm still doing the same amount of exercise – aerobics or aerobic-type exercise twice a week, resistance exercise once or twice a week and walking at least 4 km almost every day. I still eat plenty of vegetables and salad. I'm still eating the same amount of bread – about one slice a day. But I have at least halved my alcohol intake – some weeks I don't have any. I'm eating less pasta and rice. I'm eating less fruit – sticking to the two pieces a day, sometimes three. But the biggest change is that I'm eating the required amount of protein twice a day. When I get hungry, the hunger pangs are much less severe, and do not last as long, so I can control my eating habits much better.

'My cholesterol has gone down almost a point already, from 6.7 to 5.8. I think I'll be able to continue to follow the principles of the Diet for the rest of my life, as it's no effort.'
– *Elizabeth*

'I've just started the CSIRO Total Wellbeing Diet. I'm not obese, but my New Year's resolution is to lose 5 kilos. I'd just like to thank the CSIRO for coming up with a great diet that's easy to follow. I'm not at all hungry.

'I used to eat a lot more meat when I was not on your diet, and find I have a lot more energy now. I don't want chocolates, biscuits or chips any more. I am exercising, and drinking a lot more water. My husband is on the Diet with me and needs to lose 15 kilos. I'm sure that with this book he will.'
– *Renata*

'I've been on the CSIRO Total Wellbeing Diet for 11½ weeks now and have lost 10 kilos. I was only slightly overweight to begin with (70 kilos, height 163 cm), and was initially aiming for a loss of 5 kilos. I've managed this by following the Diet and walking for 50 minutes every morning. I haven't really been a 'dieter', preferring instead to follow the sensible principles of diet and exercise to lose weight. The CSIRO Total Wellbeing Diet appealed to me for this reason. I've found it easy to follow and stick to, and am now allowing myself one night a week to eat what takes my fancy and accompany this with a few glasses of wine – and I'm still losing! A spin-off benefit has been the money I've saved by preparing all my food at home and taking my lunch to work. Overall I've increased my intake of fruit and vegetables, low-GI carbohydrates and fish, and the meat I have is lean. So, my diet is now much more balanced and sustainable over the long term.'
– *Debra*

the CSIRO exercise plan

The CSIRO Exercise Plan has two components: an aerobic walking program; and a resistance tube exercise program.

When beginning your exercise program, it is best to start at a low intensity and gradually increase over time, particularly if you have not been active for a long time. If you try to do too much too soon, you run the risk of frustration and injury. Also remember to see your doctor before starting any exercise program, and be patient when looking for results. Too often, people begin an exercise program expecting to see immediate outward changes. You don't get out of shape or put on weight overnight, so it is unrealistic to think you can get back into shape overnight.

aerobic walking program

For the 12-week walking/jogging program described here, we recommend that you start with 10–20 minutes a day, 3 days a week (particularly if you have been inactive for a long time), and progress to 45–60 minutes a day 4–5 times a week as you become fitter and continue through the program (see table pages 58–9). You should always go at your own pace: this is your program, and it's important to increase the amount and intensity of your walking only when you feel comfortable.

It is vital to ensure that you walk at an optimal intensity, to achieve the greatest benefits from the program safely and effectively. If you walk at too low a rate, your body will reap little or no benefits, and you may become frustrated at not seeing the results you expect. On the other hand, if you try to walk at too high a rate, you'll tire too quickly and risk injury. An easy and reliable way to monitor your exercise intensity is to think about your level of exertion and monitor your breathing difficulty; you should exercise so that it feels vigorous and challenging but not strenuous. For most, this will be a brisk walk, but for others it will be a jog. A simple way of ensuring that your stress level is not too high is to use the 'talk test'. At a moderate intensity, you should still be able to talk comfortably with your exercise partner. If, however, you are completely out of breath, you may be working too hard. On the other hand, if you can still sing your favourite song, you may not be working hard enough and might need to pick up the pace. If you're walking with a partner, take care not to get distracted by your conversation. Remember, it's not supposed to be a Sunday-afternoon stroll.

As you become fitter, your heart rate will decrease and your breathing will become easier. So if you continue to walk at the same speed over and over, eventually you will reach a point where your program will no longer stress your aerobic system. But if you maintain a suitable level of exertion (do the talk test to check), you will ensure that you are applying a constant load to your cardiovascular system each time you exercise. Eventually you may need to jog rather than walk in order to achieve the same cardiovascular load.

It is also important to remember that if you do not have time to complete your exercise in one continuous exercise session, the same health benefits can be achieved by accumulating the same amount of exercise in several intermittent bouts of at least 10 minutes each during the day. So, instead of completing one continuous 45-minute walk, you might find it easier to fit three 15-minute walks into your daily schedule (such as in the morning, at lunchtime and in the evening). This will make it much easier to incorporate regular physical activity into your lifestyle.

10 000 steps per day

Most of us average between 3000 and 6000 steps a day in our day-to-day activities. However, scientific research has shown that walking an average of 10 000 steps a day can help protect us against obesity and yield a number of health-related benefits, such as weight-loss, blood pressure reduction, lower blood cholesterol levels and increased glucose tolerance. In fact, the greater the number of steps we take each day, the lower our weight, body-fat levels and waist circumference will become.

You can measure the number of steps you take each day by using a pedometer. It is not essential to use a pedometer for your walking program, but they can help to motivate you to be active every day and to monitor your progress. Pedometers can be purchased from most sports or electronics shops for $40–50. They clip onto your belt or waistband and count the number of steps you have taken, or kilometres you have walked, and some even calculate the amount of energy you have expended.

The best way to use a pedometer is first to wear it for a week, during your day-to-day activities, then average the number of steps you have taken each day, to see how active or inactive you currently are. Once you know how many steps you take each day, you can set yourself realistic goals for increasing that number. You should aim, of course, for 10 000 steps a day, but don't try to increase to this level straightaway, particularly if you have just discovered that you are doing nowhere near that. Instead, increase your number of daily steps by 10 per cent or 500 steps a week, tracking your progress as you go, until you reach your target. This method really works.

Even though pedometers can be useful, remember that clocking up the 10 000 steps a day does not necessarily guarantee that you will meet your physical activity requirements. This is because many of those 10 000 steps can be low-intensity physical activity (such as walking around the office or house). While all of this activity is beneficial, bursts of moderate activity of at least 10 minutes at a time will provide much greater benefit. Most people find it easier to achieve their goal of 10 000 steps a day by undertaking at least 30 minutes a day of moderate-intensity physical activity. It may well be difficult to achieve 10 000 steps without this extra activity!

resistance tube exercise program

A convenient and effective way to undertake a complete strength-training workout of all your major muscle groups is to use a resistance tube. Resistance tubes can be purchased for about $30 from most sports and fitness shops or over the Internet, and provide a great workout in the convenience of your home or office. Because they are light and easy to carry around, you can even take them with you when you travel, so there is never any excuse not to exercise!

Resistance tubes rely on elasticity to create resistance, and can easily be manipulated to suit your level of strength. They are great because they are an easy and safe way to get started with strength training – there is no weight or dumbbell to drop or lose control of, and no unnecessary pressure on the spine.

For the complete CSIRO Exercise Plan, the resistance tube program given here should be used in conjunction with your aerobic walking program.

Equipment

To get started, you will need the following equipment:

- a resistance tube – which has two handles attached by an elasticised tube. They are available in different colours, to indicate the resistive strength of the tube, which is determined by its thickness. Select a band with a suitable level of intensity for your current strength. Some tubes contain latex, to which some people are allergic, but latex-free tubes are available.
- a door attachment – for a number of important exercises that require the resistance tube to be secured at its centre point. The door attachment is fastened in a closed door to provide a secure anchor point for the tube. It can be purchased wherever resistance tubes are available. If you don't have a door attachment or a suitable doorway, the resistance tube can instead be placed around a fixed object, such as a bedpost or table leg, at the desired height.

Safety considerations

Before you commence your resistance tube exercise program, make sure you have considered the following points.

- Before each workout, check for holes or worn spots in the tubing. Replace the tube if you see any tears; damaged tubes can break under tension.
- Do your workout on carpet, wooden floors or grass, that is, on any non-slip surface except asphalt or cement – abrasive surfaces can tear your tube.
- Ensure you have plenty of free space around you to exercise properly
- Wear comfortable, supportive athletic shoes, not sandals or dress shoes. Do not try to exercise with bare feet.
- Make sure the tubing is secured underfoot or on a secure anchor before you begin each exercise. When using the door attachment, remember either to lock the door or to tell those around you what you're doing, so that they don't inadvertently use the door.

Preliminary instructions

- Before starting the program make sure you have read the instructions for each exercise carefully.
- Always maintain correct body alignment and posture, as shown in the photographs (it may be easier to exercise in front of a mirror). Incorrect posture can cause injury.

- For all standing exercises, keep your knees slightly bent, your feet shoulder-width apart, your weight distributed evenly and your toes pointing forwards.
- Your abdominal muscles should be pulled in, your chest expanded, your head and neck held straight and your eyes focused straight ahead.
- Perform the exercise program in the given order, in a circuit-type fashion, with a short rest period (about 1 minute) between each exercise.
- When you are required to complete more than one set for each exercise, repeat the same exercise for the desired number of sets, taking a 30–60 second break between each set. Then move on to the next exercise in the workout.
- Complete the program 2–3 times a week. Allow at least one rest day between each resistance tube exercise session, to allow sufficient recovery. It's a great idea to alternate your strength-training days with your walking program.
- Always start each exercise with slight tension on the tube. The tension will increase through the movement.
- You should perform each exercise at a level where it feels somewhat difficult and where you feel fatigued on the last repetition of each set.
- Those exercises where the tube is anchored away from your body become easier to perform as you become stronger. To maintain the intensity and resistance of the exercise, stand further away from the point of attachment to create greater tension in the tube.
- Only increase the level of resistance when you can comfortably complete the specified number of repetitions.
- Remember to keep breathing – never hold your breath. Breathe out during the initial motion of the exercise (that is, when you are pulling on the tube) and breathe in on the return phase.
- Perform the exercises in a slow and controlled manner by taking about 4 seconds for each repetition, that is, about 2 seconds to pull on the tube and 2 seconds to return to the starting position.
- Remember, if you can't complete the entire workout in one session, you can break it into two sessions during the day. Do half in the morning and half at night.
- You can even complete your resistance tube workout while watching TV. The important thing is that you do it!
- A day or two after your initial workout, you can become sore, particularly if you're not used to that type of exercise. It's just your body's way of letting you know that the exercise workout was effective and that you worked hard.
- After the first few workouts the delayed muscle soreness will dissipate as your muscles get used to the exercise.
- If you feel any muscle or joint pain, stop exercising immediately and seek medical attention.

the CSIRO Exercise Plan

	aerobic walking program	resistance tube program
week 1	10–20 minute walk 3 times a week	1 set each exercise 8–12 repetitions each set 30–60 second rest between each set twice a week
week 2	10–20 minute walk 3 times a week	1–2 sets each exercise 8–12 repetitions each set 30–60 second rest between each set twice a week
week 3	20–30 minute walk 3 times a week	1–2 sets each exercise 8–12 repetitions each set 30–60 second rest between each set twice a week
week 4	20–30 minute walk 4 times a week	2 sets each exercise 12–15 repetitions each set 30–60 second rest between each set twice a week
week 5	30–40 minute walk 4 times a week	2 sets each exercise 12–15 repetitions each set 30–60 second rest between each set twice a week
week 6	30–40 minute walk 4 times a week	2–3 sets each exercise 12–15 repetitions each set 30–60 second rest between each set twice a week

	aerobic walking program	resistance tube program
week 7	45–60 minute walk 4 times a week	2–3 sets each exercise 12–15 repetitions each set 30–60 second rest between each set 2–3 times a week
week 8	45–60 minute walk 4 times a week	2–3 sets each exercise 12–15 repetitions each set 30–60 second rest between each set 2–3 times a week
week 9	45–60 minute walk 4–5 times a week at least	2–3 sets each exercise 15–20 repetitions each set 30–60 second rest between each set 2–3 times a week
week 10	45–60 minute walk 4–5 times a week at least	2–3 sets each exercise 15–20 repetitions each set 30–60 second rest between each set 2–3 times a week
week 11	45–60 minute walk 4–5 times a week at least	2–3 sets each exercise 15–20 repetitions each set 30–60 second rest between each set 2–3 times a week
week 12	45–60 minute walk 4–5 times a week at least	2–3 sets each exercise 15–20 repetitions each set 30–60 second rest between each set 2–3 times a week

resistance tube exercise program

1

LATERAL RAISES

1   Stand upright, with the centre of the tube placed securely under the arch of one foot.

2   Grip one handle in each hand and stand with your arms at your sides, your thumbs pointing forward.

3   Stabilise your torso by tightening your abdominal muscles and, with your elbows slightly bent, slowly lift your arms up and out to the side, away from your body, with your palms facing the floor, pausing when your arms are at about shoulder height and parallel to the floor.

4   Slowly lower your arms back down to their starting position.

5   Repeat.

    As you become stronger, maintain the exercise intensity by standing on the tube with both feet. Move your feet further apart for even greater resistance.

2
SQUATS WITH TURNED-OUT KNEES

1   Stand with your feet apart and your legs turned out slightly at the hips, your toes pointing outwards. Make sure your knees are in line with your feet.

2   With your weight evenly distributed over your toes and heels, and your feet firmly planted, particularly the back half of your feet, and with your hands on your hips, tighten your abdominal muscles and bend your knees, keeping your back straight.

3   Squat down as if you are going to sit in a chair, until your knees are at an angle of about 90 degrees or at a comfortable angle, ensuring they do not bend more than 90 degrees. Make sure that both knees remain directly in line with your feet and do not extend over your toes. If they do, allow your hips to go further back.

4   Slowly straighten to your starting position.

5   Repeat.

As you become stronger and the squats become easier to perform, maintain the exercise intensity and resistance by performing the squat exercise using the resistance tube as shown on page 62.

RESISTED SQUATS (ADVANCED)

1   Stand upright with your feet about shoulder-width apart and both on the centre of the tube.

2   Grip one handle in each hand and hold them as close to the front of your shoulders as possible, with your elbows directly beside your body.

3   Perform the squat exercise as described for Squats with Turned-out Knees (see page 61).

Moving your feet wider apart will make the exercise harder, or closer will make it easier.

3

SEATED ROW

1   Sit on the floor and grasp one handle in one hand.

2   Wrap the tubing around a bedpost or have the door attachment anchored close to ground level, and grab the other handle with your other hand.

3   Sit far enough away from the anchor, with your back straight (don't slouch!), for there to be tension on the tube when your arms are extended straight in front of you and parallel to the floor.

4   Extend your legs in front of you with your knees slightly bent and your feet hip-width apart.

5   Squeezing your shoulder blades together, slowly pull the handles until your elbows form right angles.

6   Bring your elbows back as far as you can, keeping your back straight and relaxed, your elbows at shoulder level and your arms parallel to the floor.

7   Slowly let your arms return to their starting position.

8   Repeat.

Alternatively, the rowing exercise can be performed standing up, as described on page 64.

STANDING ROW

1 Place the centre of the tube around a fixed object or the door attachment at chest height.

2 Facing the tube, with a handle in each hand, stand upright with your feet shoulder-width apart, your knees slightly bent and your toes pointing forwards.

3 Stand away from the anchor so that your arms are straight in front of you, in line with the tubing and parallel to the floor, the tube under light tension.

4 Tighten your abdominal muscles to stabilise your torso then squeeze your shoulder blades together and slowly pull the handles backwards and outwards, with your elbows straight out from your shoulders.

5 Bring your elbows back as far as you can, your back straight and relaxed, keeping your elbows up at shoulder level and your arms parallel to the floor.

6 Slowly let your arms return to their starting position.

7 Repeat.

To make this exercise harder, sit or stand further back, or make it easier by standing closer to the anchor point.

4

CHEST PRESS

1   Place the centre of the tube around a fixed object or the door attachment at chest height.

2   Facing away from the anchor, place your feet shoulder-width apart, with one foot in front of the other, and bend your knees slightly.

3   Grip one handle in each hand and bring your elbows up to your sides, just below shoulder height, with your thumbs at your armpits and your upper arms parallel to the floor. Make sure there is some resistance in the tube.

4   Stabilise your torso by tightening your abdominal muscles, then slowly push your hands forward until your arms are almost completely extended and your hands come together in front of you.

5   Slowly return your hands to their starting position.

6   Repeat.

To make this exercise harder, stand further away from the anchor point, or move closer to make it easier.

5

LUNGES

1 Stand up straight with your hands on your hips and your feet hip-width apart.

2 Keeping your abdominal muscles tightened and your head and chest straight, take a step backwards with your right leg and land on the ball of your foot.

3 Keeping your hips square, your back as straight as possible and your knees directly in line with your ankles, slowly bend your knees, lowering your body so your right knee almost touches the floor. Your left knee should not bend more than 90 degrees, nor go over your left foot. If it does, take a bigger step back.

4 Slowly begin to stand back up, bringing your right leg forwards and placing it next to your left.

5 Switch to the left foot and repeat this movement.

6 Repeat.

As you become stronger and the lunges become easier to perform, maintain the exercise intensity by performing the lunge exercise with the resistance tube, as follows.

RESISTED LUNGES (ADVANCED)

1 Stand upright with one foot on the centre of the tube and the handles held in front of your shoulders. The tube should be inside your elbows and your forearms vertical.

2 Squeezing your shoulder blades together and keeping your head and chest forward, perform the Lunge exercise as described opposite, moving the foot that is not standing on the tube.

6

LATERAL PULL-DOWN

1   Place the centre of the tube around a fixed object or the door attachment above head height. You may need a towel to kneel on.

2   Kneel on the floor, facing the anchor, and grip one handle of the tube in each hand, with your palms facing forward and your arms straight out and angled slightly upwards, in line with the tubing. Make sure the tubing is taut.

3   Stabilise your torso by tightening your abdominal muscles, then slowly start pulling the handles back and down, bending your elbows.

4   Keeping your back straight and ensuring your body does not sway during the exercise, continue pulling on the handles until your hands reach your sides.

5   Slowly return your arms to their starting position.

6   Repeat.

To make this exercise harder, move further away from the anchor point, or make it easier by moving closer. Alternatively, you could substitute the Upright Row, as follows.

UPRIGHT ROW

1 Stand upright with both feet on the centre of the tube, about shoulder-width apart.

2 Grip one handle of the tube in each hand, and hold your hands in front of your hips, both arms extended straight down to the floor.

3 Keeping your abdominal muscles tightened, and leading with your elbows, raise both arms up and out to the sides until your hands come towards your chin. Ensure your back remains still throughout.

4 Slowly lower your arms to their starting position.

5 Repeat.

As you become stronger, maintain the exercise intensity by standing with your feet further apart, to reduce the length of the tube.

7

TRICEPS PRESS

1 Place the centre of the tube around a fixed object or the door attachment above head height.

2 Stand facing the anchored tube with your feet shoulder-width apart and one foot in front of the other, as pictured.

3 Grip one handle of the tube in each hand.

4 Place your elbows at your sides – where they should stay throughout the exercise – and your hands in front of your chest, with the tube slightly taut.

5 Stabilise your torso by tightening your abdominal muscles, then, with your palms facing downwards and your shoulders back, straighten your arms by moving your hands towards your thighs, ensuring your elbows do not move away from your sides.

6 Slowly relax your arms to their starting position.

7 Repeat.

Alternatively, you could substitute the Arm Press, as follows.

ARM PRESS

1 Start by standing with your right foot in front of the left, with the tubing under the right foot.

2 Grip one handle of the tube in each hand and bend forwards at the waist, holding the right handle at the knee of your right leg and the left handle at your waist.

3 Keeping the rest of your body stable, with your palm in and your elbow tucked in next to your body, extend the left arm by pulling the left handle behind you and past your hip. You can either follow the movement of your arm with your head, or keep looking straight ahead.

4 Slowly bend your left elbow back to its starting position, keeping your upper arm stable.

5 Repeat.

6 Switch to the other side and repeat.

8

BICEPS CURLS

1 Stand up straight with one foot on the centre of the tube and your feet hip-width apart.

2 Grip one handle of the tube in each hand and hold your arms extended at your sides.

3 Keeping your abdominal muscles tightened, raise your hands towards your shoulders until your elbows are fully bent, with your palms facing your shoulders.

4 Slowly extend your arms to their starting position.

5 Repeat.

As you become stronger, maintain the exercise intensity by standing with both feet on the centre of the tube (move your feet further apart for increased resistance), or by attaching the centre of the tube to a fixed object at floor level and stepping back for the required tension.

9

ABDOMINAL CRUNCH

1   Lie flat on your back on a mat or towel with your knees bent and the soles of your feet on the floor, hip-width apart.

2   Straighten your arms and rest your palms on the tops of your thighs, or cross your arms over your chest.

3   Leading with the chest, keeping your head and neck straight and ensuring that the motion comes from your abdominals and remains smooth, lift your upper body off the floor and towards your knees, to an angle of no more than 30 degrees to the floor (not a full sit-up). Focusing on a point on the ceiling will help you to keep your head and neck in a fixed position throughout the exercise.

4   Slowly uncurl until you are back in your starting position.

5   Repeat.

part three

menu plans for the CSIRO Total Wellbeing Diet

week one

The following pages contain detailed 12-week menu plans. Follow these to the letter, or substitute your favourite foods for those listed – provided you substitute an equal quantity of the same food group, for example 200 g low-fat yoghurt for 250 ml low-fat milk, or 1 cup salad leaves for 1 cup steamed broccoli.

For Week One we have included the nutritional breakdown of each meal for each day. This should give you an idea of an easy and simple way to include the relevant quantities of each food group each day. Use this template as a guide when creating your own menu plans, but remember, your plans can be as creative and personal as you like, as long as you are eating the required volume of each food group each day. Remember to include an extra dairy unit as a snack each day (see below).

daily snack

* Eat one extra dairy unit each day as a snack to ensure adequate calcium intake. Select any food from the dairy options on page 8.

	breakfast
day 1	1 unit cereal, 1 unit dairy, 1 unit fruit e.g. ¾ cup (40 g) high-fibre breakfast cereal 250 ml low-fat milk 1 sliced banana
day 2	1 unit cereal, 1 unit dairy, 1 unit fruit e.g. ¾ cup (40 g) high-fibre breakfast cereal 250 ml low-fat milk 1 piece fresh fruit
day 3	1 unit cereal, 1 unit dairy, 1 unit fruit e.g. 40 g instant oats 250 ml low-fat milk 30 g sultanas or raisins
day 4	1 unit cereal, 1 unit dairy, 1 unit fruit e.g. ¾ cup (40 g) high-fibre breakfast cereal 250 ml low-fat milk 1 piece fresh fruit
day 5	1 unit cereal, 1 unit dairy, 2 units fruit e.g. Bircher Muesli with Bran (see p 116) 200 g low-fat yoghurt
day 6	1 unit cereal, 1 unit dairy, 2 units fruit e.g. Bircher Muesli with Bran (see p 116) 200 g low-fat yoghurt
day 7	1 unit bread, 1 unit cereal, 1 unit fruit, 1 unit fats e.g. 2 slices wholegrain toast 2 tsp light margarine Vegemite 1 piece fresh fruit

• see pages 220–4 for weekly shopping lists

lunch	dinner	day's total units

...unit protein, 1 unit bread, 1 unit fruit,
...unit vegetables, 1 unit fats
...g. Open tuna sandwich
    (1 slice wholegrain bread
    2 tsp light margarine
    100 g tinned tuna
    ½ cup salad leaves)
    1 piece fresh fruit
	2 units protein, 1 unit bread, 1 unit dairy,
	2 units vegetables, 2 units fats
	e.g. 200 g beef: Beef Kebabs with Currant Couscous
	    & Harissa (see p 166)
	    1 cup salad with oil-free salad dressing
	    200 g low-fat dairy dessert
		3 units protein
		2 units bread
		1 unit cereal
		3 units dairy*
		2 units fruit
		2½ units vegetables
		3 units fats

...unit protein, 2 units bread,
...unit vegetables, 1 unit fats
...g. Roast pork & salad sandwich
    (2 slices wholegrain bread
    2 tsp light margarine
    100 g roast pork with apple sauce
    slices of onion
    ½ cup chopped salad leaves)
	2 units protein, 1 unit dairy, 1 unit fruit,
	2 units vegetables, 2 units fats
	e.g. 200 g chicken: Roasted Chicken with Thyme,
	    Red Onions & Butternut Pumpkin (see p 156)
	    ½ cup steamed broccoli & carrot
	    150 g tinned fruit
	    200 g low-fat dairy dessert
		3 units protein
		2 units bread
		1 unit cereal
		3 units dairy*
		2 units fruit
		2½ units vegetables
		3 units fats

...unit protein, 2 units bread, ½ unit vegetables,
...units fats
...g. Chicken roll
    (1 wholegrain bread roll [70 g]
    100 g cooked chicken
    40 g avocado
    ½ cup salad leaves)
	2 units protein, 1 unit dairy, 1 unit fruit,
	2 units vegetables, 1 unit fats
	e.g. 200 g fish: coat white fish fillets with Lemon
	    Pepper rub (see *Book 1*, p 125) & 1 tsp oil,
	    then grill or barbecue
	    2 cups salad with oil-free salad dressing
	    150 g tinned fruit
	    200 g low-fat dairy dessert
		3 units protein
		2 units bread
		1 unit cereal
		3 units dairy*
		2 units fruit
		2½ units vegetables
		3 units fats

...unit protein, 2 units bread, 1½ units vegetables,
...units fats
. Turkey sandwich
    (2 slices wholegrain bread
    100 g turkey with cranberry sauce
    40 g avocado)
    1½ cups salad with oil-free salad dressing
	2 units protein, 1 unit dairy, 1 unit fruit,
	1 unit vegetables, 1 unit fats
	e.g. 200 g lamb: Polenta-crumbed Lamb Chops
	    with Zucchini & Feta (see p 188)
	    1 piece fresh fruit
	    100 g low-fat dairy dessert
		3 units protein
		2 units bread
		1 unit cereal
		3 units dairy*
		2 units fruit
		2½ units vegetables
		3 units fats

...unit protein, 2 units bread, 1 unit vegetables,
...units fats
. Egg & tuna roll
    (1 wholegrain bread roll [70 g]
    1 hard-boiled egg
    50 g tinned tuna
    1 cup salad leaves
    40 g avocado)
	2 units protein, 1 unit dairy,
	1½ units vegetables, 1 unit fats
	e.g. 200 g seafood: Stir-fried Chilli Plum Calamari with
	    Crunchy Vegetable Salad (see p 140)
	    200 g low-fat dairy dessert
		3 units protein
		2 units bread
		1 unit cereal
		3 units dairy*
		2 units fruit
		2½ units vegetables
		3 units fats

...unit protein, 2 units bread, ½ unit vegetables,
...units fats
. Sardines on toast
    (2 slices wholegrain toast
    1 tsp pesto
    100 g sardines
    slices of tomato
    ½ cup salad leaves)
	2 units protein, 1 unit dairy,
	2 units vegetables, 1 unit fats
	e.g. 200 g beef: coat sirloin steaks in 1 tsp oil,
	    then grill or barbecue
	    Roasted Cherry Tomatoes & Asparagus
	    with Lemon Thyme (see p 202)
	    200 g low-fat dairy dessert
		3 units protein
		2 units bread
		1 unit cereal
		3 units dairy*
		2 units fruit
		2½ units vegetables
		3 units fats

...unit protein, 1 unit dairy,
2 units vegetables, ½ unit fats
. Chicken salad
    (100 g cooked chicken
    1½ cups chopped salad vegetables
    10 g avocado
    25 g feta
    oil-free salad dressing)
	2 units protein, 1 unit bread, 1 unit dairy,
	1 unit fruit, 1 unit vegetables, 1½ units fats
	e.g. 200 g lamb: Indian Lamb Patties (see p 187)
	    ⅓ cup cooked white & brown rice
	    1 cup chopped vegetables stir-fried in
	    1½ tsp sesame oil
	    Baked Apples with Cinnamon & Ricotta (see p 206)
		3 units protein
		2 units bread
		1 unit cereal
		3 units dairy*
		2 units fruit
		2½ units vegetables
		3 units fats

week two

daily snack

* Eat one extra dairy unit each day as a snack to ensure adequate calcium intake. Select any food from the dairy options on page 8.

	breakfast	lunch	dinner
day 1	40 g instant oats cooked with 250 ml low-fat milk 30 g sultanas or raisins	Turkey sandwich (2 slices wholegrain bread with 100 g turkey, cranberry sauce, 40 g avocado & ½ cup rocket leaves)	200 g beef: Soy & Ginger Beef with Broccolini (see p 168) 1 cup bok choy & carrots stir-fried in 1 tsp oil 150 g tinned fruit with 200 g low-fat dairy dessert
day 2	¾ cup (40 g) high-fibre breakfast cereal with 250 ml low-fat milk 1 piece fresh fruit	Salmon sandwich (2 slices wholegrain bread with 2 tsp light margarine, 100 g tinned salmon, 60 g avocado, slices of tomato & onion & ½ cup salad leaves) 200 g low-fat yoghurt	200 g chicken: marinate chicken breast in Tandoori marinade (see *Book 1*, p 124) & grill or barbecue 2 cups steamed squash & Brussels sprouts 150 g tinned fruit
day 3	2 slices wholegrain toast with 2 tsp light margarine & 25 g cheese Smoothie made with 1 piece fresh fruit & 250 ml low-fat milk	Open tandoori chicken sandwich (1 slice wholegrain bread with 2 tsp light margarine, 100 g tandoori chicken & slices of cucumber) 1 cup salad with oil-free salad dressing	200 g fish: Steamed Salmon with Thai Sauce (see p 143) 1½ cups bok choy, cauliflower & broccolini stir-fried in 1 tsp oil 150 g tinned fruit
day 4	¾ cup (40 g) high-fibre breakfast cereal with 250 ml low-fat milk 1 piece fresh fruit	2 wholegrain crispbreads with 50 g ham, 1 hard-boiled egg, 2 tsp pesto, slices of tomato & onion & ½ cup rocket leaves 200 g low-fat yoghurt 1 piece fresh fruit	200 g beef: Beef Stroganoff (see p 173) ⅓ cup cooked rice 1 cup steamed peas & green beans & pumpkin mash
day 5	¾ cup (40 g) high-fibre breakfast cereal with 125 ml low-fat milk 100 g low-fat yoghurt 1 piece fresh fruit	Chicken & salad sandwich (2 slices wholegrain bread with 1 tsp sun-dried tomato pesto, 100 g cooked chicken, bean sprouts & ½ cup salad leaves) 150 g fresh fruit salad	200 g fish: pan-fry white fish fillets in 1 tsp oil & top with Olive Gremolata (see *Book 1*, p 120) 2 cups steamed green beans, corn & carrot 200 g low-fat dairy dessert
day 6	40 g instant oats cooked with 250 ml low-fat milk 75 g tinned fruit	Salmon salad (100 g tinned salmon with 1 cup chopped salad vegetables & 1 tbsp oil-free mayonnaise) 2 wholegrain crispbreads	200 g lamb: Lamb Biryani (see p 193) 1½ cups steamed squash, peas & carrot 150 g tinned fruit with 200 g low-fat dairy dessert
day 7	¾ cup (40 g) high-fibre breakfast cereal with 250 ml low-fat milk 1 egg (poached, boiled or scrambled) 1 slice wholegrain toast 1 piece fresh fruit	Open tuna sandwich (1 slice wholegrain bread with 2 tsp light margarine, 50 g tinned tuna, 1 tbsp oil-free mayonnaise & 1 cup baby spinach leaves)	200 g veal: Veal Escalopes with Fennel, Spinach & Olives (see p 176) 150 g tinned fruit with 200 g low-fat dairy dessert

• see pages 220–4 for weekly shopping lists

week three

daily snack
* Eat one extra dairy unit each day as a snack to ensure adequate calcium intake. Select any food from the dairy options on page 8.

	breakfast	lunch	dinner
day 1	¾ cup (40 g) high-fibre breakfast cereal with 125 ml low-fat milk 30 g sultanas or raisins 100 g low-fat yoghurt	Egg & salad sandwich (2 slices wholegrain bread with 2 tsp light margarine, 2 hard-boiled eggs, 1 tbsp oil-free mayonnaise, curry powder & ½ cup salad leaves)	200 g fish: Poached Blue-eye with Peperonata & Basil (see p 143) 1 cup steamed green beans, snow peas & carrot 150 g tinned fruit with 200 g low-fat dairy dessert
day 2	2 slices wholegrain toast with 2 tsp light margarine & Vegemite 1 piece fresh fruit 200 g low-fat yoghurt	Bacon, Egg & Mushroom Bake (see p 121) 1 piece fresh fruit	200 g beef: marinate diced beef fillets in Beef or Lamb marinade (*Book 1*, p 124), thread onto skewers, then barbecue ⅓ cup cooked couscous or brown rice 1½ cups steamed pumpkin, peas & broccoli
day 3	2 slices wholegrain toast with low-joule jam 1 piece fresh fruit 1 low-fat cafe latte or low-fat cappuccino	Bacon, Egg & Mushroom Bake (see p 121) 1 cup salad with oil-free dressing 100 g low-fat yoghurt	200 g lamb: Lamb Saag (see p 189) ⅓ cup cooked polenta or brown rice 1 cup steamed carrot, peas & broccoli 1 piece fresh fruit
day 4	¾ cup (40 g) high-fibre breakfast cereal with 250 ml low-fat milk 225 g fresh fruit salad	Tuna & salad roll (1 wholegrain bread roll [70 g] with 100 g tinned tuna, 40 g avocado, slices of cucumber & ½ cup salad leaves)	200 g pork: Pork Cutlet with Avocado, Orange & Beetroot Salad (see p 162) 1 cup pumpkin mash 200 g low-fat dairy dessert
day 5	¾ cup (40 g) high-fibre breakfast cereal with 250 ml low-fat milk 1 piece fresh fruit	Ham & egg salad sandwich (2 slices wholegrain bread with 3 tsp light margarine, 50 g ham, 1 hard-boiled egg, 50 g cottage cheese, mustard, slices of tomato & ½ cup salad leaves)	200 g veal: Lemon Cumin Veal Cutlets with Parsnip Mash & Baby Green Beans (see p 176) ½ cup steamed baby carrots 150 g tinned fruit
day 6	¾ cup (40 g) high-fibre breakfast cereal with 250 ml low-fat milk 1 piece fresh fruit	Chicken roll (1 wholegrain bread roll [70 g] with 1 tsp pesto, 100 g cooked chicken, 40 g avocado, slices of tomato & red onion & ½ cup salad leaves)	200 g fish: marinate white fish fillets in Chilli & Lime (see *Book 1*, p 123) & grill 2 cups steamed bok choy & broccolini 150 g fresh fruit salad with 200 g low-fat dairy dessert
day 7	Grilled cheese & tomato on toast (2 slices wholegrain toast with 2 tsp light margarine, 25 g cheddar, slices of tomato & cracked pepper) 1 piece fresh fruit	Beef, Spinach & Pumpkin Salad (see p 132) 1 crispbread	200 g lamb: Italian Lamb Meatloaf (see p 189) 1 cup steamed corn, green beans & carrot 150 g fresh fruit salad with 200 g low-fat dairy dessert

• see pages 220–4 for weekly shopping lists

week four

daily snack

* Eat one extra dairy unit each day as a snack to ensure adequate calcium intake. Select any food from the dairy options on page 8.

	breakfast	lunch	dinner
day 1	40 g instant oats cooked with 250 ml low-fat milk 1 piece fresh fruit	Chicken wrap (1 wholemeal Lebanese flatbread [70 g] with 100 g cooked chicken, chutney, bean sprouts, slices of tomato & ½ cup rocket leaves) 150 g fresh fruit salad 200 g low-fat yoghurt	200 g beef: coat rump steaks with Lemon Pepper (see *Book 1*, p 125) & 1 tsp oil, then grill or barbecue Grilled Eggplant with Tomatoes & Balsamic Vinegar (see p 202) 1 cup salad with oil-free salad dressing
day 2	¾ cup (40 g) high-fibre breakfast cereal with 250 ml low-fat milk 1 piece fresh fruit	Tuna salad (100 g tinned tuna with 1 cup salad leaves, olives, slices of tomato & cucumber & oil-free salad dressing)	200 g chicken: Chargrilled Pesto Chicken with Tabouleh (see p 159) 1 cup steamed squash, peas & carrot 150 tinned fruit with 200 g low-fat dairy dessert
day 3	¾ cup (40 g) high-fibre breakfast cereal with 250 ml low-fat milk 1 piece fresh fruit	4 wholegrain crispbreads with 4 tsp light margarine, 50 g smoked salmon, 1 hard-boiled egg, capers, slices of tomato & red onion & ½ cup baby spinach leaves	200 g fish: Fish Stew with Tomato & Basil (see p 147) 1 cup salad with oil-free salad dressing 150 g fresh fruit salad with 200 g low-fat dairy dessert
day 4	¾ cup (40 g) high-fibre breakfast cereal with 250 ml low-fat milk 1 piece fresh fruit	Toasted ham sandwich (2 slices wholegrain bread with 50 g ham, 60 g avocado & 25 g cheese) 1 cup salad with oil-free salad dressing	200 g lamb: marinate diced lamb fillets in Greek-style marinade (see *Book 1*, p 124), thread onto skewers, then barbecue 1½ cups steamed green beans, zucchini & carrot 150 g fresh fruit salad
day 5	40 g instant oats cooked with 250 ml low-fat milk 1 piece fresh fruit	Chicken & salad wrap (1 wholemeal Lebanese flatbread [70 g] with 100 g cooked chicken, 3 tsp sun-dried tomato pesto, olives & ½ cup rocket leaves) 1 cup salad with oil-free salad dressing	200 g fish: Steamed Salmon with Thai Sauce (see p 143) 1 cup steamed peas, carrot & broccolini 1 piece fresh fruit 200 g low-fat yoghurt
day 6	1 slice wholegrain toast with ⅓ cup baked beans 200 g low-fat yoghurt	Sweet Corn & Crab Soup (see p 126) 2 wholegrain crispbreads 1 piece fresh fruit	200 g lamb: Moussaka (see p 193) 1 cup salad with oil-free salad dressing 150 g tinned fruit
day 7	1 egg (poached, boiled or scrambled) with ½ tomato pan-fried in ½ tsp oil 1 slice wholegrain toast with 1 tsp light margarine 1 low-fat cafe latte or low-fat cappuccino	Salmon & salad roll (1 wholegrain roll [70 g] with 50 g tinned salmon, chopped onion & ½ cup salad leaves) 1 piece fresh fruit 200 g low-fat dairy dessert	200 g beef: Classic Roast Beef (see p 173) 150 g tinned fruit with 100 g low-fat dairy dessert

• see pages 220–4 for weekly shopping lists

week five

daily snack

* Eat one extra dairy unit each day as a snack to ensure adequate calcium intake. Select any food from the dairy options on page 8.

	breakfast	lunch	dinner
day 1	Bircher Muesli with Bran (see p 116) 100 g low-fat yoghurt	Open turkey sandwich (1 slice wholegrain bread with 2 tsp light margarine, 100 g turkey, 25 g Swiss cheese, cranberry sauce & ½ cup salad leaves)	200 g beef: Beef & Vegetable Pasta Bake (see p 172) 1 cup salad with oil-free dressing
day 2	Bircher Muesli with Bran (see p 116) 200 g low-fat yoghurt	Roast pork & salad roll (1 wholegrain bread roll [70 g] with 2 tsp light margarine, 100 g roast pork, apple sauce & ½ cup salad leaves) 200 g low-fat yoghurt	200 g fish: coat salmon steaks with 1 tsp oil, then barbecue & top with Miso Sesame Sauce (see *Book 1*, p 121) 2 cups steamed snow peas, cauliflower & asparagus
day 3	Bircher Muesli with Bran (see p 116) 200 g low-fat yoghurt	Chicken roll (1 wholegrain bread roll [70 g] with 2 tsp light margarine, 100 g cooked chicken, chutney, slices of tomato & onion & ½ cup watercress)	200 g lamb: Chermoula Lamb Fillet with Avocado & Coriander Salsa (see p 190) 2 cups steamed carrot & asparagus 200 g low-fat dairy dessert
day 4	¾ cup (40 g) high-fibre breakfast cereal with 250 ml low-fat milk 1 piece fresh fruit	Rosemary Lamb with Olive & Feta Salad (see p 131) 2 wholegrain crispbreads with 1 tsp pesto	200 g chicken: Marinated Chicken with Steamed Greens (see p 156) ⅓ cup cooked brown rice 150 g fresh fruit salad with 100 g low-fat dairy dessert
day 5	¾ cup (40 g) high-fibre breakfast cereal with 250 ml low-fat milk 1 small glass orange juice	Spicy Lamb Burger with Tzatziki (see p 187) with 1 extra slice wholegrain bread 200 g low-fat yoghurt	200 g fish: Stir-fried Chilli Plum Calamari with Crunchy Vegetable Salad (see p 140) 1 cup broccoli, cauliflower & carrot stir-fried in 2 tsp sesame oil 150 g tinned fruit
day 6	2 slices wholegrain toast with low-joule jam Smoothie made with 1 piece fresh fruit & 250 ml low-fat milk	Open tuna sandwich (1 slice wholegrain bread with 100 g tinned tuna, slices of tomato & ½ cup salad leaves) 200 g low-fat dairy dessert	200 g lamb: coat lean lamb chops in 1 tsp oil, then grill or barbecue Pumpkin Mash with Cabbage & Spring Onions (see p 201) 150 g fresh fruit salad
day 7	¾ cup (40 g) high-fibre breakfast cereal with 250 ml low-fat milk 30 g sultanas or raisins	Open egg & salad sandwich (1 slice rye bread with 2 tsp light margarine, 2 hard-boiled eggs, 2 tsp oil-free mayonnaise, slices of onion, 20 g avocado & ½ cup salad leaves) 200 g low-fat yoghurt	200 g beef: Beef Vindaloo (see p 174) 2 cups steamed spinach, pumpkin & green beans 150 g tinned fruit

• see pages 220–4 for weekly shopping lists

week six

daily snack

* Eat one extra dairy unit each day as a snack to ensure adequate calcium intake. Select any food from the dairy options on page 8.

	breakfast	lunch	dinner
day 1	¾ cup (40 g) high-fibre breakfast cereal with 250 ml low-fat milk 1 piece fresh fruit	Curried egg roll (1 wholegrain bread roll [70 g] with 2 tsp light margarine, 2 hard-boiled eggs, 1 tbsp oil-free mayonnaise, curry powder & ½ cup salad leaves)	200 g fish: marinate tuna steaks in Ginger Soy (see *Book 1*, p 123) & pan-fry in 1 tsp oil 2 cups broccoli & carrot stir-fried in 1 tsp oil 150 g tinned fruit with 200 g low-fat dairy dessert
day 2	40 g instant oats cooked with 250 ml low-fat milk 150 g tinned fruit	Ham sandwich (2 slices wholegrain bread with 2 tsp light margarine, 50 g ham, 1 hard-boiled egg, 20 g avocado, slices of tomato & ½ cup salad leaves)	200 g beef: Barbecued Steak with Artichoke & Herb Salad (see p 171) 1 cup steamed cauliflower & broccoli 150 g tinned fruit with 200 g low-fat yoghurt
day 3	¾ cup (40 g) high-fibre breakfast cereal with 250 ml low-fat milk 1 piece fresh fruit	Tuna sandwich (2 slices wholegrain bread with 2 tsp light margarine, 100 g tinned tuna, finely chopped celery & ½ cup salad leaves)	200 g chicken: Roasted Chicken with Thyme, Red Onions & Butternut Pumpkin (see p 156) 1 cup steamed green beans & carrot 1 piece fresh fruit with 200 g low-fat yoghurt
day 4	Bircher Muesli with Bran (see p 116) 100 g low-fat yoghurt 1 low-fat cafe latte or low-fat cappuccino	Roast pork sandwich (2 slices wholegrain bread with 2 tsp light margarine, 100 g roast pork, pickles, slices of onion & cucumber & ½ cup salad leaves)	200 g lamb: coat lamb fillets in 1 tsp oil, then grill or barbecue & top with Parsley Relish (see *Book 1*, p 120) 2 cups steamed cauliflower & green beans 200 g low-fat dairy dessert
day 5	Bircher Muesli with Bran (see p 116) 200 g low-fat yoghurt	Chicken wrap (1 wholemeal Lebanese flatbread [70 g] with 100 g cooked chicken, 2 tsp pesto, slices of tomato & 1 cup baby spinach leaves)	200 g fish: Sesame Ocean Trout with Mixed Mushrooms (see p 144) 200 g low-fat dairy dessert
day 6	Bircher Muesli with Bran (see p 116) 14 g flaked almonds 100 g low-fat yoghurt	Salmon salad (100 g tinned salmon with 1 cup salad vegetables & oil-free salad dressing) 2 wholegrain crispbreads 100 g low-fat yoghurt	200 g beef: Beef Stroganoff (see p 173) ⅓ cup cooked white & brown rice ½ cup steamed spinach, squash & green beans 200 g low-fat dairy dessert
day 7	2 eggs (poached, boiled or scrambled) 1 slice wholegrain toast with 2 tsp light margarine 1 low-fat cafe latte or low-fat cappuccino	2 wholegrain crispbreads with 2 tsp light margarine & 25 g cheese ½ cup salad with oil-free salad dressing 1 piece fresh fruit	200 g lamb: Lamb Tagine (see p 194) 1 cup steamed carrot, pumpkin & green beans 150 g fresh fruit salad with 100 g low-fat dairy dessert

• see pages 220–4 for weekly shopping lists

week seven

daily snack

* Eat one extra dairy unit each day as a
snack to ensure adequate calcium intake.
Select any food from the dairy options
on page 8.

	breakfast	lunch	dinner
day 1	¾ cup (40 g) high-fibre breakfast cereal with 250 ml low-fat milk 1 piece fresh fruit	Tuna salad (100 g tinned tuna with 1½ cups salad leaves, olives, slices of tomato & cucumber, 2 tsp pine nuts & oil-free salad dressing 1 slice wholegrain bread	200 g beef: Beef Kebabs with Currant Couscous & Harissa (see p 166) 1 cup steamed carrot, peas & green beans 150 g fresh fruit salad with 200 g low-fat dairy dessert
day 2	¾ cup (40 g) high-fibre breakfast cereal with 250 ml low-fat milk 1 piece fresh fruit	Chicken & salad wrap (1 wholemeal Lebanese flatbread [70 g] with 100 g cooked chicken, 40 g avocado, ½ cup salad leaves & 2 tsp oil-free mayonnaise)	200 g seafood: Stir-fried King Prawns (see p 140) ½ cup steamed pumpkin 1 piece fresh fruit 200 g low-fat dairy dessert
day 3	¾ cup (40 g) high-fibre breakfast cereal with 250 ml low-fat milk 1 piece fresh fruit	Tuna sandwich (2 slices wholegrain bread with 2 tsp light margarine, 100 g tinned tuna, 1 tbsp oil-free mayonnaise, bean sprouts & ½ cup salad leaves) 1 piece fresh fruit with 100 g low-fat yoghurt	200 g lamb: coat lean lamb chops with Lemon Pepper (see *Book 1*, p 125) & 1 tsp oil, then grill or barbecue Cauliflower with Leeks & Parmesan (see p 201) & 1 cup steamed beans
day 4	¾ cup (40 g) high-fibre breakfast cereal with 250 ml low-fat milk 1 low-fat cafe latte or low-fat cappuccino	2 wholegrain crispbreads with 2 tsp light margarine 1 cup salad with ⅓ cup chick peas, 100 g tinned salmon, 1 chopped apple & oil-free salad dressing	200 g chicken: Coq au Vin (see p 160) ½ cup steamed carrot & peas 1 piece fresh fruit 100 g low-fat yoghurt
day 5	40 g instant oats cooked with 250 ml low-fat milk 150 g tinned fruit	Turkey & salad pita (1 wholemeal pita bread [70 g] with 100 g turkey, cranberry sauce, 40 g avocado & 1 cup salad leaves) 1 piece fresh fruit	200 g fish: Steamed Salmon with Thai Sauce (see p 143) 1½ cups steamed broccoli, corn & cauliflower tossed in 1 tsp sesame oil 200 g low-fat dairy dessert
day 6	¾ cup (40 g) high-fibre breakfast cereal with 20 g nuts & 250 ml low-fat milk 1 piece fresh fruit	Bean salad (⅓ cup tinned three-bean mix with 50 g ham, 1 hard-boiled egg, 1 cup chopped salad veg & oil-free dressing) 2 wholegrain crispbreads 1 piece fresh fruit	200 g beef: marinate diced beef fillets in Beef marinade (see *Book 1*, p 124), thread onto skewers, then barbecue 1½ cups steamed peas, pumpkin & zucchini 200 g low-fat yoghurt
day 7	¾ cup (40 g) high-fibre breakfast cereal with 250 ml low-fat milk 1 slice wholegrain toast with 2 tsp light margarine & 1 boiled egg	1 slice wholegrain toast with 50 g sardines, slices of tomato & ½ cup rocket leaves 1 piece fresh fruit	200 g lamb: Moussaka (see p 193) ½ cup steamed carrot and zucchini 150 g tinned fruit

• see pages 220–4 for weekly shopping lists

week eight

daily snack

* Eat one extra dairy unit each day as a snack to ensure adequate calcium intake. Select any food from the dairy options on page 8.

	breakfast	lunch	dinner
day 1	2 slices wholegrain toast with 25 g cheese 100 g low-fat yoghurt	2 wholegrain crispbreads with 2 tsp light margarine, 100 g tinned tuna & oil-free mayonnaise 1 cup salad with oil-free salad dressing 1 piece fresh fruit	200 g beef: Beef & Eggplant 'Cannelloni' (see p 172) ½ cup salad with balsamic vinegar 150 g fresh fruit salad
day 2	¾ cup (40 g) high-fibre breakfast cereal with 250 ml low-fat milk 1 piece fresh fruit	Open pastrami sandwich (1 slice wholegrain bread with 2 tsp pesto, 50 g pastrami, pickles, 25 g cheese, slices of red onion & ½ cup salad leaves)	200 g chicken: Marinated Chicken with Steamed Greens (see p 156) ⅓ cup cooked brown rice 1 cup steamed broccolini, zucchini & peas 150 g tinned fruit
day 3	1 slice wholegrain toast with 1 poached egg 200 g low-fat yoghurt 1 piece fresh fruit	Chicken sandwich (2 slices wholegrain bread with 2 tsp light margarine, 50 g cooked chicken, chutney, slices of tomato & cucumber & ½ cup rocket leaves)	200 g fish: marinate white fish fillets in Ginger Soy (see *Book 1*, p 123) & grill or barbecue 2 cups snow peas, broccolini & carrot stir-fried in 2 tsp oil 1 piece fresh fruit with 200 g low-fat yoghurt
day 4	¾ cup (40 g) high-fibre breakfast cereal with 250 ml low-fat milk 1 small glass orange juice	Ham roll (1 wholegrain bread roll [70 g] with 2 tsp light margarine, 2 tsp pesto, 50 g ham, 1 hard-boiled egg & ½ cup salad leaves)	200 g lamb: Indian Lamb Patties (see p 187) 2 cups steamed zucchini & squash 150 g tinned fruit with 200 g low-fat dairy dessert
day 5	¾ cup (40 g) high-fibre breakfast cereal with 250 ml low-fat milk 1 piece fresh fruit	Chicken & salad pita (1 wholemeal pita bread [70 g] with 2 tsp light margarine, 100 g cooked chicken, 1 tbsp hummus & 1 cup rocket leaves)	200 g fish: Steamed Bream with Lemon & Capers (see p 147) 150 g tinned fruit with 200 g low-fat dairy dessert
day 6	2 wholemeal crumpets with 2 tsp light margarine & low-joule jam 1 low-fat cafe latte or low-fat cappuccino	Tuna salad (100 g tinned tuna with 25 g cheese, 1 cup salad, slices of tomato & 1 tbsp oil-free mayonnaise) 2 wholegrain crispbreads 1 piece fresh fruit	200 g veal: Veal Escalopes with Fennel, Spinach & Olives (see p 176) 150 g fresh fruit salad with 100 g low-fat dairy dessert
day 7	¾ cup (40 g) high-fibre breakfast cereal with 250 ml low-fat milk 1 piece fresh fruit	Chicken salad (100 g cooked chicken with ⅓ cup chick peas, slices of tomato & onion, 25 g Swiss cheese, 1 cup salad leaves & oil-free salad dressing)	200 g lamb: rub a leg of lamb with 1 tbsp oil & herbs, then roast 1 baked potato 1½ cups baked carrots, onion & zucchini 150 g tinned fruit

• see pages 220–4 for weekly shopping lists

week nine

daily snack

* Eat one extra dairy unit each day as a snack to ensure adequate calcium intake. Select any food from the dairy options on page 8.

	breakfast	lunch	dinner
day 1	¾ cup (40 g) high-fibre breakfast cereal with 250 ml low-fat milk 1 piece fresh fruit	Salmon sandwich (2 slices wholegrain bread with 2 tsp light margarine, 100 g tinned salmon, mustard, 25 g cheese, slices of pickled onion & ½ cup salad leaves)	200 g veal: coat veal cutlets with Lemon Pepper (see *Book 1*, p 125) & 1 tsp oil, then grill or barbecue Roasted Cherry Tomatoes & Asparagus with Lemon Thyme (see p 202) 1 piece fresh fruit
day 2	¾ cup (40 g) high-fibre breakfast cereal with 250 ml low-fat milk 1 piece fresh fruit	Chicken & avocado roll (1 wholegrain bread roll [70 g] with 100 g cooked chicken, 40 g avocado & ½ cup rocket leaves) 1 cup salad with oil-free salad dressing	200 g fish: Fish Stew with Tomato & Basil (see p 147) 1 cup steamed zucchini, pumpkin & peas 150 g tinned fruit with 200 g low-fat dairy dessert
day 3	1 slice wholegrain toast with ⅓ cup baked beans 150 g fresh fruit salad with 100 g low-fat yoghurt	Tomatoes Stuffed with Tuna, Basil & Spinach (see p 138) 2 wholegrain crispbreads ½ cup rocket leaves 100 g low-fat yoghurt	200 g lamb: Lamb & Rosemary Sausages (see p 184) ½ cup pumpkin mash ½ cup steamed corn & peas 1 piece fresh fruit
day 4	¾ cup (40 g) high-fibre breakfast cereal with 250 ml low-fat milk 1 piece fresh fruit	Salmon sandwich (2 slices rye bread with 100 g tinned salmon, slices of tomato & 1 cup salad leaves) 1 piece fresh fruit	200 g chicken: Baked Chicken Breast Stuffed with Parsley, Lemon & Pine Nuts (see p 154) 1 cup (5 spears) steamed asparagus 1 cup steamed pumpkin & zucchini
day 5	40 g instant oats cooked with 250 ml low-fat milk 1 piece fresh fruit	Pastrami roll (1 wholegrain bread roll [70 g] with 2 tsp pesto, 50 g pastrami, pickles, 25 g cheese, slices of tomato & red onion & ½ cup salad leaves)	200 g fish: coat white fish fillets with Fish Rub (see *Book 1*, p 125) & 1 tsp oil, then grill or barbecue 2 cups steamed squash, carrot & snow peas 150 g tinned fruit
day 6	¾ cup (40 g) high-fibre breakfast cereal with 250 ml low-fat milk 1 piece fresh fruit	Tuna wrap (1 wholemeal Lebanese flatbread [70 g] with 100 g tinned tuna, 2 tsp sun-dried tomato pesto & 1 cup baby spinach leaves)	200 g lamb: Polenta-crumbed Lamb Chops with Zucchini & Feta (see p 188) ½ cup salad with oil-free salad dressing 150 g fresh fruit salad with 100 g low-fat yoghurt
day 7	¾ cup (40 g) high-fibre breakfast cereal with 250 ml low-fat milk 1 piece fresh fruit	Ham, egg & salad sandwich (2 slices wholegrain bread with 3 tsp light margarine, 50 g ham, 1 hard-boiled egg, mustard, slices of tomato & ½ cup salad leaves)	200 g beef: Sichuan Pepper Sirloin with Broccoli & Capsicum (see p 168) 1 cup steamed bok choy 150 g tinned fruit with 200 g low-fat dairy dessert

• see pages 220–4 for weekly shopping lists

week ten

daily snack

* Eat one extra dairy unit each day as a snack to ensure adequate calcium intake. Select any food from the dairy options on page 8.

	breakfast	lunch	dinner
day 1	Bircher Muesli with Bran (see p 116) 100 g low-fat yoghurt 1 low-fat cafe latte or low-fat cappuccino	Roast beef roll (1 wholegrain bread roll [70 g] with 2 tsp light margarine, 100 g roast beef, horseradish, slices of tomato & red onion & ½ cup watercress)	200 g fish: Poached Blue-eye with Peperonata & Basil (see p 143) 1 cup steamed peas, zucchini & carrot 200 g low-fat dairy dessert
day 2	Bircher Muesli with Bran (see p 116) 100 g low-fat yoghurt 1 low-fat cafe latte or low-fat cappuccino	Open tuna & salad sandwich (1 slice wholegrain bread with 2 tsp light margarine, 100 g tinned tuna, slices of cucumber & gherkins & ½ cup salad leaves)	200 g beef: Beef & Vegetable Pasta Bake (see p 172) 1 cup salad with oil-free salad dressing 100 g low-fat yoghurt
day 3	Bircher Muesli with Bran (see p 116) 100 g low-fat yoghurt	2 slices wholegrain toast with 2 tsp light margarine & 100 g sardines 1 cup salad with 20 g avocado & oil-free salad dressing 100 g low-fat yoghurt	200 g chicken: marinate chicken in Tandoori marinade (see *Book 1*, p 124) & grill 1½ cups steamed spinach, pumpkin & zucchini 200 g low-fat dairy dessert
day 4	40 g instant oats cooked with 250 ml low-fat milk & 75 g tinned fruit 100 g low-fat yoghurt	Egg & salad sandwich (2 slices rye bread with 2 tsp light margarine, 2 hard-boiled eggs, slices of tomato & red onion & ½ cup salad leaves) 1 cup salad with oil-free salad dressing	250 ml low-joule vegetable soup 200 g lamb: Spiced Lamb Salad with Orange, Coriander & Red Onion (see p 182) 150 g fresh fruit salad
day 5	¾ cup (40 g) high-fibre breakfast cereal with 250 ml low-fat milk 1 piece fresh fruit	Chicken & salad sandwich (2 slices wholegrain bread with 4 tsp light margarine, 100 g cooked chicken, slices of tomato & 1 cup salad leaves)	250 ml low-joule vegetable soup 200 g fish: Sesame Ocean Trout with Mixed Mushrooms (see p 144) 150 g fresh fruit salad with 200 g low-fat yoghurt
day 6	2 slices wholegrain toast with 25 g cheese & Vegemite 200 g low-fat yoghurt	Lemon Tuna Patties (see p 122) 1 cup salad with oil-free salad dressing 2 wholegrain crispbreads 1 piece fresh fruit	200 g beef: grill or barbecue steaks in 1 tsp oil 1½ cups steamed Brussels sprouts, cauliflower & carrot 150 g tinned fruit
day 7	1 slice wholegrain toast with 2 tsp light margarine, 25 g cheese, ⅓ cup baked beans & slices of tomato 1 small glass orange juice	Chicken salad (100 g cooked chicken with 1 cup chopped salad vegetables, 25 g feta, 20 g avocado & oil free salad dressing) 1 piece fresh fruit	200 g lamb: Lamb Tagine (see p 194) 1 cup steamed snow peas, squash & carrot

• see pages 220–4 for weekly shopping lists

week eleven

daily snack

* Eat one extra dairy unit each day as a
snack to ensure adequate calcium intake.
Select any food from the dairy options
on page 8.

	breakfast	lunch	dinner
day 1	¾ cup (40 g) high-fibre breakfast cereal with 250 ml low-fat milk 1 piece fresh fruit	Salmon salad (100 g tinned salmon with 1 cup chopped salad vegetables, 50 g low-fat cheese, 40 g avocado & 1 tbsp oil-free mayonnaise) 2 wholegrain crispbreads	200 g beef: Beef Vindaloo (see p 174) 1½ cups steamed spinach, green beans & carrot 150 g tinned fruit
day 2	40 g instant oats cooked with 250 ml low-fat milk 150 g fresh fruit salad	Roast pork roll (1 wholegrain bread roll [70 g] with 3 tsp light margarine, 100 g roast pork, slices of tomato & red onion, apple sauce & 1 cup salad leaves)	200 g veal: Lemon Cumin Veal Cutlets with Parsnip Mash & Baby Green Beans (see p 176) 1 piece fresh fruit with 200 g low-fat dairy dessert
day 3	¾ cup (40 g) high-fibre breakfast cereal with 250 ml low-fat milk 1 piece fresh fruit	Chicken roll (1 wholegrain bread roll [70 g] with 2 tsp light margarine, 100 g cooked chicken, chutney, slices of tomato & cucumber & ½ cup rocket leaves)	200 g fish: pan-fry fish fillets in 1 tsp oil & top with Parsley Relish (see *Book 1*, p 120) 2 cups steamed snow peas, broccoli & carrot 150 g tinned fruit with 200 g low-fat dairy dessert
day 4	¾ cup (40 g) high-fibre breakfast cereal with 250 ml low-fat milk 1 piece fresh fruit	Chicken wrap (1 wholemeal Lebanese flatbread [70 g] with 3 tsp pesto, 100 g cooked chicken, 25 g feta, slices of tomato & 1 cup baby spinach leaves)	200 g beef: Soy & Ginger Beef with Broccolini (see p 168) ½ cup steamed bok choy & green beans 150 g fresh fruit salad
day 5	1 slice wholegrain toast with 2 tsp light margarine & 1 poached egg Smoothie made with 1 piece fresh fruit & 250 ml low-fat milk	Egg & bean salad (½ cup tinned three-bean mix, 1 hard-boiled egg, 1 cup chopped salad vegetables & oil-free salad dressing) 2 wholegrain crispbreads	250 ml low-joule vegetable soup 200 g fish: Steamed Bream with Lemon & Capers (see p 147) 150 g tinned fruit with 200 g low-fat dairy dessert
day 6	2 slices wholegrain toast with 1 scrambled egg & slices of grilled tomato 100 g low-fat yoghurt 1 piece fresh fruit	Tuna salad (50 g tinned tuna with 25 g feta, ½ cup tinned corn, ½ cup chopped tomato & green beans, ½ cup salad leaves & oil-free salad dressing) 2 wholegrain crispbreads	200 g chicken: coat chicken breast with 1 tsp oil & grill or barbecue, then top with Parsley Relish (see *Book 1*, p 120) Zucchini with Spinach & Goat's Cheese (p 198) 1 piece fresh fruit
day 7	¾ cup (40 g) high-fibre breakfast cereal with 250 ml low-fat milk 15 g sultanas or raisins	Open turkey sandwich (1 piece wholegrain bread with 100 g turkey, cranberry sauce, 25 g Swiss cheese & 1 cup salad leaves)	200 g lamb: Lamb Biryani (see p 193) 1½ cups steamed zucchini & carrot 1 piece fresh fruit

• see pages 220–4 for weekly shopping lists

week twelve

daily snack

* Eat one extra dairy unit each day as a snack to ensure adequate calcium intake. Select any food from the dairy options on page 8.

	breakfast	lunch	dinner
day 1	Bircher Muesli with Bran (see p 116) 100 g low-fat yoghurt 1 low-fat cafe latte or low-fat cappuccino	Chicken sandwich (2 slices wholegrain bread, 2 tsp pesto, 100 g cooked chicken, 50 g low-fat cheese, slices of tomato & 1 cup salad leaves)	250 ml low-joule vegetable soup 200 g fish: Sesame Ocean Trout with Mixed Mushrooms (see p 144)
day 2	Bircher Muesli with Bran (see p 116) 200 g low-fat yoghurt	Egg & salad sandwich (2 slices wholegrain bread with 4 tsp light margarine, 2 hard-boiled eggs, 1 tbsp oil-free mayonnaise, slices of spring onion & ½ cup salad leaves)	200 g lamb: coat lean lamb chops with Lamb Rub (see *Book 1*, p 125) & 1 tsp oil, then grill or barbecue 2 cups steamed pumpkin, squash & zucchini 200 g low-fat dairy dessert
day 3	Bircher Muesli with Bran (see p 116) 100 g low-fat yoghurt 1 low-fat cafe latte or low-fat cappuccino	Salmon salad (100 g tinned salmon with chopped onion, 1 cup chopped salad vegetables & oil-free salad dressing) 4 wholegrain crispbreads with 4 tsp light margarine	200 g pork: Pork Loin with Tomato & Sage (see p 162) 200 g low-fat yoghurt
day 4	¾ cup (40 g) high-fibre breakfast cereal with 250 ml low-fat milk 1 piece fresh fruit	Open chicken sandwich (1 slice wholegrain bread with 2 tsp light margarine, 100 g cooked chicken, chutney, 25 g feta & slices of tomato) 1 cup salad with oil-free salad dressing	200 g lamb: Lamb Saag (see p 189) ½ cup cooked white & brown rice ½ cup steamed green beans 150 g tinned fruit
day 5	40 g instant oats cooked with 250 ml low-fat milk 1 piece fresh fruit	Egg sandwich (2 slices wholegrain bread with 2 tsp light margarine, 2 hard-boiled eggs, slices of cucumber, bean sprouts & ½ cup salad leaves) 1 piece fresh fruit	200 g fish: marinate white fish fillets in Chilli & Lime (see *Book 1*, p 123) & grill 2 cups broccoli, peas & carrot stir-fried in 2 tsp oil 200 g low-fat yoghurt
day 6	¾ cup (40 g) high-fibre breakfast cereal with 250 ml low-fat milk 1 piece fresh fruit	Chicken pita (1 wholemeal pita bread [70 g] with 100 g chicken, 40 g avocado, 1 tbsp oil-free mayonnaise & ½ cup salad leaves)	200 g beef: Barbecued Steak with Artichoke & Herb Salad (see p 171) 1 cup steamed zucchini & carrot 150 g fresh fruit salad with 200 g low-fat yoghurt
day 7	¾ cup (40 g) high-fibre breakfast cereal with 250 ml low-fat milk 1 piece fresh fruit	Corn Fritters with Smoked Salmon & Spinach (see p 122)	250 ml low-joule vegetable soup 200 g lamb: Chermoula Lamb Fillet with Avocado & Coriander Salsa (see p 190) 150 g tinned fruit with 100 g low-fat dairy dessert

• see pages 220–4 for weekly shopping lists

part four

recipes for the CSIRO Total Wellbeing Diet

by Heidi Flett

The following 10 pages contain ideas for items that can be easily packed into a lunchbox for school or work. Fresh foods – including sandwiches and salads – and packaged food are both included, with ideas ranging from quick-and-easy lunches that can be thrown together in the morning rush, to meats, vegies or bakes that have been prepared the day or night before.

lunchbox ideas

sandwiches, wraps and rolls

Sandwiches would have to be the easiest and best-loved lunchbox meal, but it's all too easy to run out of ideas and end up with the same ham, cheese and tomato day after day. Here are some different types of ingredients you can use, including a number of different breads. Turn over for suggested flavour combinations.

With such a wide variety of breads on offer, you shouldn't run out of options. Most of the breads shown here are available in supermarkets or delis, but don't be afraid to experiment with different breads from your local bakery.

multigrain loaf

baguette

ciabatta

turkish bread

wholemeal loaf

sourdough roll

pita

wraps

rye roll

sunflower-seed roll

Make sure you buy only low-salt, high-fibre varieties – wholegrain, wholemeal, seed loaves or white high-fibre should be your breads of choice.

Herbs are a fantastic way to jazz up a sandwich, wrap or roll. Pick a few leaves, chop or tear them roughly, then sprinkle them over your filling.

Another way to add variety and a flavour boost to sandwiches, wraps and rolls is to include a spread with your fillings. Choose from those shown here, or any spread from the Condiments section of the free list on page 9.

dill

basil

flat-leaf parsley

chives

oregano

mint

rosemary

thyme

chutney

mustard

pesto

taramasalata

hummus

oil-free mayonnaise

pickles

beetroot dip

sun-dried tomato pesto

Here are a few this-goes-with-that ideas for sandwiches, wraps and rolls to get you started. The beauty of these lunches is that everyone in the family can easily make up a different one to suit their individual tastes. Please note that all sandwiches, wraps and rolls should contain up to 100 g protein food (1 unit). This can be as tinned tuna or salmon, cooked cold chicken, other meats or eggs. Always cook extra meat in the evenings and use the leftovers in your lunches; this will help you keep costs down and will mean you don't need to buy large amounts of expensive (and salty) processed meats. A hard-boiled egg plus up to 50 g cold chicken, fish or red meat can keep costs down without compromising on nutrition.

SANDWICHES

Sandwiches come in all shapes and sizes – use the following as inspiration for your own creations, but make sure you stick to your daily bread allowance: 2 × 35 g slices wholegrain bread (2 units).

100 g cooked chicken
1 tablespoon oil-free mayonnaise
⅓ sliced avocado, drizzled
    with lemon juice
½ cup rocket (arugula)

100 g sliced turkey
cranberry sauce
½ cup baby spinach

100 g rare roast beef
roasted capsicum
artichoke hearts
½ cup rocket (arugula)

100 g tinned tuna
1 tablespoon oil-free
    mayonnaise
¼ cup finely diced celery
½ sliced tomato

100 g hot salami
50 g low-fat feta
½ sliced tomato
½ cup rocket (arugula)

Note: Although these photos include red meat, there is no need to eat red meat at lunchtime. Tuna, salmon, chicken, turkey and eggs are all excellent options for your lunch protein-food requirements.

ROLLS AND BAGELS

Perfect on a picnic, or for lunch almost anywhere, rolls are a welcome variation on the usual sandwich. Each roll should be 70 g (2 units bread) and can be stuffed with as many delicious fillings as will fit!

100 g rare roast beef
mustard
bean sprouts
½ sliced tomato
½ cup rocket (arugula)

100 g cooked chicken
1–3 teaspoons pesto
25 g Swiss cheese
½ cup rocket (arugula)

50 g smoked salmon
1 hard-boiled egg
sliced red (Spanish) onion
capers

1 sliced tomato
50 g bocconcini
basil

WRAPS

Wraps are lighter and less doughy than other types of bread, and can make a refreshing change. Flavours include plain, spinach and tomato, and sizes vary. As with pitas, check the packet and make sure you choose wraps to suit your daily bread allowance. Tuck the wetter ingredients, such as tomato, into the centre of the wrap, otherwise it will be soggy by lunchtime.

PITAS

Tasty and convenient, pitas are another easy low-dough bread option and are available from most supermarkets and delis. They come in various sizes: make sure you choose one to suit your daily bread allowance of 70 g (2 units).

100 g cooked chicken
beetroot dip
½ cup rocket (arugula)

100 g pastrami
pickles
½ cup rocket (arugula)

100 g cooked lamb
yoghurt mint dressing
(see page 109)
1 diced tomato
½ cup baby spinach

salads

Salads make delicious take-to-work lunches, and can be as hearty or as light as you like. The best thing about them is that they can use up all the leftovers from meals the day before – and are often tastier as a result!

There are many varieties of salad leaves, from hearty, leafy greens, including spinach and witlof, to lighter, crisper lettuces, such as cos and iceberg. Cabbage also makes a lovely base for a salad.

Additional greens, such as alfalfa, watercress and other sprouts, add great texture and crunch.

cos lettuce

iceberg lettuce

witlof

green cabbage

butter lettuce

red cabbage

bean spro

mesclun

rocket

watercress

Trim salad leaves where necessary, to remove the harder, more fibrous parts of the leaf or stem. Also wash the leaves; rinse under cold running water and spin in a salad spinner or dry on a clean tea towel or cloth.

A good dressing is a very important part of a salad, but it's crucial not to toss the salad in advance, or it will be wilted and soggy by lunchtime. Mix up the dressing in a small container and tuck this into the corner of your lunchbox, then, at lunchtime, add the dressing to the salad and toss the lot together.

There are plenty of tasty low-fat salad dressings on the market, but if you want to make your own, turn to the Sauces, Marinades & Rubs chapter in *Book One*, or try these easy dressings (making note of their fat or dairy content):

classic vinaigrette: ⅓ cup olive oil, 2 teaspoons Dijon mustard, 2 teaspoons good-quality white-wine vinegar, freshly ground black pepper to taste

thai: 2 tablespoons lime juice, 1 tablespoon fish sauce, 1 tablespoon soy sauce, 1 crushed clove garlic, 1 seeded and chopped red chilli

yoghurt mint dressing: 2 tablespoons low-fat natural yoghurt, 2 teaspoons mint sauce, 1 teaspoon olive oil, 2 teaspoons lemon juice

Some ingredients that are fabulous in salads, but are not on the free list, are avocado (drizzled with lemon juice to stop it discolouring), tinned fish and tinned beans, and nuts. If you include these, be sure to count the serves in your daily checklist (see page 214).

Many, many foods can go into a salad, often raw. Use the ingredients here as inspiration, or turn to the free list on page 9 for more examples.

oil

white-wine vinegar

balsamic vinegar

black pepper

garlic

wholegrain mustard

cherry tomatoes

steamed broccoli

capsicum

radishes

carrot

boiled pumpkin

steamed cauliflower

Steamed or roasted vegetables and cooked meat can really bring a salad to life. Make extra serves of your dinner recipes, then toss the leftovers through a salad for lunch the next day.

Salads can either make up the whole lunch, or be a side serve to other treats, such as a frittata or salmon fishcakes. Some of these salads contain up to 100 g protein food (1 unit). Others should be served as an accompaniment to protein-food dishes.

Making a salad couldn't be easier: just start with the basic ingredients, such as salad leaves, cabbage or roast vegetables, then add your favourite bits and pieces and, finally, make up a small container of dressing to toss with the salad when you are ready to eat. Here are a few ideas to get you thinking . . .

¼ thickly sliced roasted red
   capsicum (pepper)
2 trimmed cooked spears asparagus
½ thinly sliced roasted zucchini
   (courgette)
¼ thinly sliced roasted fennel bulb
½ clove crushed garlic
1 tablespoon thyme leaves
3 tablespoons oil-free salad dressing
½ cup baby spinach
25 g feta

100 g cooked chicken breast
⅓ cup cooked rice noodles
1 tablespoon freshly grated ginger
½ finely chopped large red chilli
¼ thinly sliced red capsicum
   (pepper)
¼ cup bean sprouts
roughly torn coriander
   (cilantro)
roughly torn mint

100 g poached chicken breast
⅓ cup cooked wild rice or brown rice
½ cup halved yellow teardrop tomatoes
1 finely sliced spring onion (scallion)
roughly chopped mint
½ cup rocket (arugula)
½ finely sliced witlof

All but the tuna salad below are perfect accompaniments to tasty leftover meat or baked treats. If necessary, package the salad separately from the leftovers, to prevent the whole lot becoming a soggy mess! And don't forget to check that you are eating up to 100 g protein food for lunch, either in the salad itself, or as part of your leftovers.

100 g cooked lamb
100 g cooked chick peas
½ cup halved cherry tomatoes
finely sliced red (Spanish) onion
roughly chopped flat-leaf
    (Italian) parsley
roughly torn mint
½ cup shredded baby spinach
⅓ cup watercress

1 cup salad leaves
1 diced tomato
1 sliced avocado, drizzled
    with lemon juice

½ cup tinned three-bean mix
100 g tinned tuna
1 diced stick celery
½ diced red capsicum (pepper)

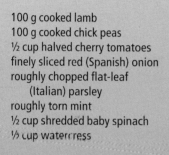

½ cup rocket (arugula)
½ cup baby spinach
50 g low-fat feta
⅓ cup olives
20 g toasted pine nuts

100 g tinned corn
½ diced red capsicum (pepper)
1 diced tomato
½ diced cucumber

bits and pieces

These pages contain ideas for other things to add to your lunchbox – bought and homemade (please refer to the recipe section, pages 115–213, for the latter). Mix and match them with sandwiches, salads and leftovers, adding units of particular food groups as your daily checklist (see page 214) allows.

Supermarkets these days offer a huge variety of packaged items. These can make life easy, while still remaining a healthy option – just make sure you check labels and purchase low-fat, low-salt alternatives where available (see pages 22–3 for more on interpreting food labels).

nuts

carrot sticks

cucumber sticks

milk

yoghurt

celery sticks

tinned corn

olives

Frûche

sultanas

dried apricots

dips

boiled eggs

tinned sardines

LEFTOVERS

Cold meat leftovers are a wonderful quick-and-easy lunch idea. When cooking dinner the night before, make more, then place your burgers (see page 187), kebabs (see page 166) or koftas (see page184) in your lunchbox with a fresh and light side salad (see page 110), a piece of fruit and/or a tub of yoghurt. Mushroom Tartlets (page 118), Corn Fritters (page 122), Salmon Fishcakes (page 138), and Bacon, Egg and Mushroom Bake (page 121) also make excellent lunchbox dishes.

QUICK REFERENCE TABLE

protein foods	dairy	fruit	vegetables
tinned tuna, tinned salmon, tinned sardines, lamb koftas, chicken kebabs, leftover roast meat, turkey, eggs	low-fat yoghurt, low-fat Frûche, low-fat dairy dessert, cheese sticks, low-fat custard	apples, oranges, bananas, grapes, mandarins, strawberries, nectarines, kiwifruit, fruit juice box, fruit packs, dried apricots, sultanas	tinned corn, carrot sticks, cucumber sticks, celery sticks

An ideal snack at any time of day, fruit is a particularly effective mid-morning or mid-afternoon pick-me-up.

fruit juice

sultanas

bananas

orange

apple

nectarines

strawberries

grapes

lamb koftas

corn fritters

chicken kebabs

bacon, egg & mushroom bake

These recipes are simple and delicious,
with an emphasis on dishes that can be
made in large quantities and eaten over
a few days, either at home, or taken to
work or school in lunchboxes.

breakfast & brunch

bran muffins

Makes 24

½ cup canola oil
½ cup honey
1 cup grated carrot
2 bananas, mashed
2 apples, unpeeled and grated
3 eggs, lightly beaten
2 cups low-fat milk
1½ cups unprocessed wheatbran
1½ cups oat bran
2 cups plain wholemeal flour
1 tablespoon baking powder
1 teaspoon ground cinnamon
1 cup pecans or walnuts, finely chopped
½ cup raisins

Preheat oven to 190°C (375°F). Lightly grease two 12-cup muffin tins.

In a large bowl, mix oil, honey, carrot, bananas, apples, eggs and milk. Stir through the two kinds of bran and let sit for 10 minutes.

In a separate bowl, combine flour, baking powder and cinnamon. Fold dry ingredients, along with pecans and raisins, through bran mixture until just mixed. Fill muffin cups two-thirds full with mixture and bake for 20 minutes, or until muffins are firm to the touch. Turn muffins out onto a wire rack to cool.

1 muffin = 1 unit cereal, 1 unit fruit, 1 unit fats

bircher muesli with bran

Serves 8 (makes 4 cups)

1 cup rolled oats
1 cup untoasted muesli
1 cup unprocessed wheatbran
2 cups hot water
2 tablespoons lemon juice
¼ cup almonds
200 g low-fat flavoured yoghurt
1 large green apple, grated
150 g seasonal fruit (berries, peaches, nectarines, bananas) per serve
2 tablespoons honey

Place the oats, muesli and bran in a large ceramic dish and pour water and lemon juice over. Allow to soak for 30 minutes. Add almonds, yoghurt and apple and stir to combine thoroughly. Cover and refrigerate overnight.

Serve with fruit and a drizzle of honey, plus extra yoghurt from your dairy allowance, if desired.

1 serve of ½ cup muesli with fruit = 1 unit cereal, 2 units fruit

leftovers
Bircher muesli keeps for – and actually improves over – about four days. Make this recipe on Sunday night and enjoy a nutritious and easy breakfast well into the week.

bircher muesli with bran

salmon & broccoli tart

LUNCH serves 4

1 quantity olive oil pastry (see page 209)
1 tablespoon olive oil
1 leek, white part only, finely sliced and washed
1 clove garlic, crushed
200 g tinned salmon, drained and flaked
1 cup broccoli, cut into small florets
50 g grated low-fat cheddar
4 eggs
½ cup low-fat milk
½ cup low-fat natural yoghurt
1 tablespoon chopped dill

Preheat oven to 200°C (390°F). Lightly grease a 20 cm fluted flan tin.

Roll out pastry and use it to line the flan tin. Cover base of pastry case with baking paper, then cover paper with dried beans or rice to stop the pastry base from puffing up during cooking. Bake for 15 minutes. Remove beans and paper and bake for a further 10 minutes. Remove from oven and reduce temperature to 160°C (320°F).

Heat oil in a large frying pan over high heat. Add leek and cook for 5 minutes, or until soft. Add garlic and cook for a further 2 minutes. Remove pan from heat and set aside.

Cover tart base with salmon, broccoli and cheese. In a small bowl, mix eggs, milk, yoghurt and dill. Add leek and garlic, season lightly and pour over tart filling.

Bake for approximately 45 minutes, or until lightly browned and puffy in the centre. Serve with a green salad.

1 serve = 1 unit protein, 1 unit bread, ½ unit dairy, ½ unit vegetables, 3 units fats

mushroom, leek & asparagus tartlets

Makes 6

12 slices wholegrain bread, crusts removed
1½ tablespoons olive oil
1 leek, white part only, finely sliced and washed
150 g Swiss brown mushrooms, quartered
250 g asparagus spears, cut into 2 cm pieces
freshly ground black pepper
25 g grated parmesan
6 eggs
½ cup low-fat milk

Preheat oven to 180°C (350°F). Lightly grease a 6-cup non-stick 'Texan' (or large) muffin tin.

Place two slices of bread on top of one another and, using a rolling pin, roll slices to a thickness of approximately 5 mm. Repeat with remaining slices. Place bread in each muffin cup, pushing down firmly to mould the bread to the tin. Bake for 5–10 minutes, or until golden. Set aside and reduce oven to 160°C (320°F).

In a heavy-based frying pan, heat oil over medium heat. Add leek and cook for 5 minutes, or until soft. Add mushrooms and cook for a further 5 minutes. Add asparagus, season with pepper then transfer to a bowl to cool.

In a separate bowl, whisk together parmesan, eggs and milk. Add the vegetables and stir to combine. Spoon the mixture into the bread cases and bake for 35 minutes, or until firm to the touch. Serve warm or cool, with a salad.

1 serve = ½ unit protein, 2 units bread, ½ unit vegetables, 1 unit fats

mushroom, leek & asparagus tartlets

bacon, egg & mushroom bake

bacon, egg & mushroom bake

LUNCH serves 4

1 tablespoon olive oil
1 red (Spanish) onion, sliced
100 g lean bacon, sliced
300 g large flat mushrooms, sliced
6 eggs
200 g low-fat natural yoghurt
1 tablespoon mustard powder
75 g grated cheddar cheese
⅓ cup roughly chopped flat-leaf (Italian) parsley
2 large ripe tomatoes, sliced

Preheat oven to 170°C (340°F). Lightly grease 4 small (or 1 large), shallow ovenproof dishes.

Heat oil in a large non-stick frying pan over medium heat. Add onion and bacon and cook for 5 minutes, or until onion is soft. Add mushrooms and cook for a further 2 minutes. Remove from heat and allow to cool.

In a bowl, lightly whisk together eggs, yoghurt and mustard powder. Add cheese, parsley and the bacon mix, and stir to combine. Pour into prepared dishes and arrange slices of tomato on top. Bake for 12–15 minutes, or until firm to the touch. (One large bake will need 20–25 minutes cooking time.) Serve with a large green salad.

1 serve = 1 unit protein, 1 unit dairy,
1 unit vegetables, 1 unit fats

variation
For a low-salt option, you could substitute cooked chicken for the bacon in this recipe.

zucchini & mint pie

LUNCH serves 4

1 tablespoon olive oil
1 onion, finely chopped
5 zucchini (courgettes), finely sliced
8 eggs
400 g low-fat natural yoghurt
½ cup roughly chopped mint
4 spring onions (scallions), finely sliced
25 g coarsely grated parmesan
25 g feta

Preheat oven to 170°C (340°F). Lightly grease a 20 cm ovenproof flan dish.

Heat oil in a large non-stick frying pan over medium heat. Add onion and sauté for 5 minutes, or until soft. Add zucchini and cook for 2 minutes. Transfer to a bowl to cool.

In a separate bowl, whisk eggs and yoghurt. Add remaining ingredients and zucchini mix, season lightly and stir to combine. Spoon mixture into prepared dish and bake for 35 minutes, or until golden and firm to the touch. Cut into slices and serve warm or cold with a crisp salad.

1 serve = 1 unit protein, 1 unit dairy,
1 unit vegetables, 1 unit fats

lemon tuna patties

LUNCH serves 4 (makes 8 patties)

300 g tinned tuna, drained
1 small red (Spanish) onion, finely chopped
2 tablespoons chopped coriander (cilantro)
2 teaspoons finely grated lemon zest
2 eggs, separated
2 tablespoons wholemeal plain flour
2 tablespoons vegetable oil

Place tuna, onion, coriander and lemon zest in a bowl and mix lightly with a fork. Add egg yolks (reserving whites for later) and continue to mix. Season lightly. Sift flour into mixture, and gently fold through.

Place the egg whites in a clean bowl and whisk until soft peaks form. Spoon the whites into the tuna mixture and gently fold through. With slightly wet hands, form the mixture into 8 patties.

Heat oil in a large non-stick frying pan over medium heat. Add patties and cook for 5 minutes each side, or until golden brown. Drain on paper towels. Serve tuna patties with a mixed-leaf salad tossed with an oil-free dressing.

1 serve = 1 unit protein, 2 units fats

lunchboxes

The tarts, bakes, pies and patties on pages 118–22 are fantastic lunchbox options, and keep well in the fridge for several days. Take them to work for lunch, and eat them cold or warm, with a side salad or vegetables (see pages 197–203).

corn fritters with smoked salmon & spinach

LUNCH serves 4 (makes 8 fritters)

1 cup wholemeal self-raising flour or 8 slices
    wholegrain bread, made into breadcrumbs
2 eggs
1 cup buttermilk
1 × 125 g tin corn, or 2 cooked corn cobs,
    kernels removed
4 spring onions (scallions), finely sliced
¼ cup roughly chopped flat-leaf (Italian) parsley
½ red capsicum (pepper), seeded and finely diced
1 tablespoon lemon juice
½ cup low-fat natural yoghurt
¼ cup roughly chopped coriander (cilantro) leaves
1 tablespoon olive oil
300 g smoked salmon
100 g baby spinach

In a large bowl, sift flour and make a well in the centre. In a separate bowl, mix eggs and buttermilk. Pour egg mixture into flour and stir to make a smooth batter. Add corn, spring onions, parsley and capsicum and fold through.

In a small bowl, mix lemon juice, yoghurt and coriander, and set aside.

Heat oil in a large non-stick frying pan over medium heat. Drop ⅓-cupfuls of mixture into the pan and cook for 3 minutes, or until golden. Turn and cook for a further 3 minutes, or until mixture is firm and set.

Serve 2 fritters per person, topped with a quarter of the smoked salmon and spinach, and drizzled with a little yoghurt dressing.

1 serve = 1 unit protein, 2 units bread, ½ unit dairy, 1 unit vegetables, 1 unit fats

corn fritters with smoked salmon & spinach

For days when a sandwich just won't do,
try these tasty lunches, but be sure to include
your daily bread allowance in other meals.

soups & salads

sweet corn & crab soup

1 tablespoon vegetable oil
1 onion, finely chopped
1 stick celery, finely diced
1 clove garlic, crushed
2 teaspoons freshly grated ginger
1 × 125 g tin corn, or 2 cooked corn cobs, kernels removed
1 litre salt-reduced chicken stock
¼ cup soy sauce
3 × 170 g tins crab meat, drained
4 spring onions (scallions), finely sliced
¼ cup roughly chopped coriander (cilantro)

Heat oil in a heavy-based saucepan over medium heat. Add onion, celery, garlic and ginger and cook for 3 minutes, or until soft. Add corn and chicken stock and bring to a boil. Reduce heat and simmer for 10 minutes. Remove from heat and allow to cool.

Transfer to a food processor and blend, leaving soup slightly chunky. Return soup to the saucepan and add soy sauce, crab meat, spring onions and coriander.

Serve sprinkled with a little extra chopped coriander, if desired.

1 serve = 1 unit protein, ½ unit vegetables, 1 unit fats

variation
You can easily use chicken instead of crab meat. Simply follow the recipe above, but add 400 g chicken mince when you add the corn and chicken stock, and omit the crab meat.

spiced red lentil & vegetable soup

2 teaspoons olive oil
1 carrot, roughly chopped
1 onion, roughly chopped
2 sticks celery, roughly chopped
1 clove garlic, crushed
1 tablespoon freshly grated ginger
1 cup dried red lentils
2 teaspoons garam masala
½ teaspoon chilli powder
1 × 400 g tin tomatoes
1 litre water
freshly ground black pepper
⅓ cup chopped coriander (cilantro)
⅓ cup chopped flat-leaf (Italian) parsley
⅓ cup low-fat natural yoghurt

Heat oil in a heavy-based saucepan over medium heat. Add carrot, onion and celery and cook for 5 minutes, or until vegetables are soft. Add garlic, ginger, lentils and spices and stir to combine. Add tomatoes and water and bring to a boil. Reduce heat and simmer for 30 minutes, or until lentils are soft. Season with pepper and stir through coriander and parsley. Spoon into bowls and serve with a dollop of yoghurt.

1 serve = 2 units bread, 1 unit vegetables, ½ unit fats

lamb shank soup with gremolata

LUNCH serves 4

2 teaspoons canola oil
3 lamb shanks (900 g with bone:
     100 g meat per person), excess fat removed
1 onion, chopped
2 carrots, chopped
1 stick celery, chopped
1 tablespoon chopped rosemary
1 clove garlic, chopped
2 large tomatoes, diced
1 litre salt-reduced beef stock
2 cups water
freshly ground black pepper
1 tablespoon finely grated lemon zest
2 tablespoons finely chopped flat-leaf (Italian) parsley

Heat oil in a heavy-based saucepan over medium heat. Add lamb shanks and cook, turning occasionally, for 10 minutes, or until golden. Remove shanks from pan and set aside. Add onion, carrots and celery to pan and cook for 5 minutes, or until soft. Return shanks to pan, add rosemary, garlic, tomatoes, stock and water, and bring to a boil. Reduce heat and simmer for 40 minutes, or until meat is almost falling off the bone.

Using a large spoon, skim off any foam, then remove shanks from soup. Allow to cool a little, then pull meat off the bone and chop roughly. Return meat to the soup, season with pepper and serve sprinkled with lemon zest and parsley.

1 serve = 1 unit protein, ½ unit vegetables, ½ unit fats

lamb shank soup with gremolata

rosemary lamb with olive & feta salad

LUNCH serves 4

1 tablespoon chopped rosemary
1 clove garlic, crushed
3 teaspoons redcurrant jelly
400 g lamb fillets, trimmed of fat and sinew
1 tablespoon olive oil
12 green olives
100 g low-fat feta
2 baby cos lettuces, outer leaves discarded, leaves separated
1 bulb fennel, finely sliced
1½ tablespoons oil-free balsamic dressing

In a small bowl, mix rosemary, garlic and redcurrant jelly. Add lamb and toss to coat thoroughly.

Heat oil in a large non-stick frying pan over medium heat. Add lamb and cook for 3 minutes each side, or until done to your liking. Remove lamb from heat, cover with foil and set aside to rest for 5 minutes.

In a large bowl, combine olives, feta, cos leaves and fennel. Toss with balsamic dressing and divide among serving plates. Slice lamb thickly on the diagonal and arrange on top of salad.

1 serve = 1 unit protein, ½ unit dairy, 1½ units vegetables, 1 unit fats

beef, spinach & pumpkin salad

LUNCH serves 4

400 g beef sirloin
300 g butternut pumpkin, diced
2 teaspoons sesame oil
1 red capsicum (pepper), seeded and sliced
3 spring onions (scallions), finely sliced
150 g baby spinach
½ cup roughly chopped coriander (cilantro)

MARINADE
¼ cup soy sauce
1 tablespoon finely sliced ginger
2 cloves garlic, roughly chopped
juice of 1 lime
2 teaspoons brown sugar

Mix marinade ingredients in a bowl. Add beef, turning to coat thoroughly, then cover bowl and allow beef to marinate for 10–15 minutes.

Preheat oven to 180°C (350°F).

Place pumpkin in a bowl with sesame oil and toss to coat. Tip pumpkin onto a baking tray and roast for 20 minutes, or until soft and golden. Add capsicum and roast for a further 5 minutes. Remove from oven and set aside.

Preheat a grill plate or barbecue grill to high. Add beef and cook for 4 minutes each side, or until done to your liking. Remove beef from heat, cover with foil and set aside to rest for 5 minutes. Slice into thin strips.

In a large bowl, toss together beef, pumpkin, capsicum, spring onions, spinach and coriander. Serve immediately.

1 serve = 1 unit protein, 1½ units vegetables, ½ unit fats

portuguese chicken salad with charred lemons

LUNCH serves 4

400 g skinless chicken breast fillets
2 lemons, halved

MARINADE
juice and finely grated zest of 1 lemon
2 cloves garlic, crushed
2 tablespoons olive oil
1 teaspoon chilli flakes

SALAD
12 spears asparagus, blanched
500 g baby potatoes, steamed and halved
100 g mixed salad leaves
2 tablespoons oil-free balsamic dressing

Mix all marinade ingredients in a large ceramic bowl. Add chicken and toss to coat thoroughly. Cover bowl and refrigerate for 30 minutes.

Preheat a grill plate or barbecue grill to high and cook chicken for 5 minutes each side, or until cooked through. Remove chicken and set aside. Cook lemons, flesh-side down, for 3 minutes.

Meanwhile, toss together all salad ingredients and divide among 4 plates. Slice chicken and arrange on top of the salad, and serve with a charred lemon half on the side of each plate.

1 serve = 1 unit protein, 2 units bread, 1 unit vegetables, 2 units fats

variation
For a tasty alternative, try chick peas in this recipe in place of the potato.

Steamed, poached, baked or stir-fried, seafood is one of the easiest and quickest meals to prepare. And with a large side serve of crisp green salad or your favourite steamed vegetables, you can practically feel it doing you good.

seafood

tomatoes stuffed with tuna, basil & spinach

LUNCH serves 4

8 medium-sized ripe tomatoes
400 g tinned tuna in spring water, drained and flaked
½ red (Spanish) onion, finely diced
⅓ cup shredded basil
1 tablespoon finely grated lemon zest
200 g low-fat ricotta
freshly ground black pepper
2 tablespoons olive oil

Preheat oven to 170°C (340°F).

Slice tops off tomatoes and carefully remove flesh with a teaspoon, reserving lids and flesh for later. Place tomato shells upside down on paper towels to drain.

Place tuna, onion, basil, lemon zest, ricotta and tomato flesh in a bowl, season well with pepper and combine thoroughly. Spoon tuna mixture into tomato shells and replace tops. Transfer tomatoes to an ovenproof dish and drizzle with olive oil. Bake for 20 minutes, or until heated through. Serve with roasted zucchini or rocket salad.

1 serve = 1 unit protein, 1 unit dairy,
1 unit vegetables, 2 units fats

salmon fishcakes with red capsicum & basil salad

LUNCH serves 4 (makes 8 patties)

400 g tinned salmon, drained
6 spring onions (scallions), finely sliced
400 g desiree potatoes, peeled, boiled and mashed
finely grated zest of 1 lemon
¼ cup roughly chopped mint
¼ cup roughly chopped flat-leaf (Italian) parsley
¼ cup plain flour
2 tablespoons vegetable oil

RED CAPSICUM & BASIL SALAD
2 roasted red capsicums (peppers), sliced
    (to roast your own capsicums, see page 190)
½ cup basil leaves
12 cherry tomatoes, halved
1 clove garlic, crushed
2 teaspoons red-wine vinegar
1 tablespoon olive oil
1 tablespoon salted baby capers, rinsed well

Combine salmon, spring onions, mashed potato, lemon zest, mint and parsley in a bowl, and roll into 8 balls. Transfer to a plate, cover with plastic wrap and refrigerate for at least 1 hour.

Preheat oven to 180°C (350°F). Sprinkle flour onto a board. Roll fish balls in flour and flatten gently. Heat half the oil in a large non-stick frying pan over medium heat. Cook 4 fishcakes for 5 minutes each side, or until golden brown. Transfer to a baking tray. Repeat with 4 remaining cakes. Bake cakes for 8 minutes, or until heated through.

Meanwhile, mix all salad ingredients in a bowl. Divide fishcakes among 4 plates and serve with the salad.

1 serve = 1 unit protein, 1 unit bread,
1 unit vegetables, 3 units fats

salmon fishcakes with red capsicum & basil salad

stir-fried king prawns

DINNER serves 4

1 green chilli, roughly chopped
¼ cup lime juice
1 tablespoon fish sauce
1 stalk lemongrass, white part only, roughly chopped
2 cloves garlic, roughly chopped
1 tablespoon vegetable oil
1 kg large uncooked prawns (shrimp)
    (200 g meat per person), peeled and de-veined
1 red capsicum (pepper), seeded and sliced
2 bunches bok choy (pak choi), chopped
2 cups bean sprouts
4 spring onions (scallions), finely sliced
⅓ cup roughly chopped coriander (cilantro)

Place chilli, lime juice, fish sauce, lemongrass and garlic in a food processor and blend to a rough paste.

Heat a wok or large frying pan over high heat. Add oil and, when smoking, add prawns. Stir-fry for 2 minutes, or until prawns have just begun to change colour. Add capsicum, bok choy and chilli paste and stir-fry for a further 3 minutes.

To serve, toss through bean sprouts, spring onion and coriander.

1 serve = 2 units protein, 1½ units vegetables,
1 unit fats

stir-fried chilli plum calamari with crunchy vegetable salad

DINNER serves 4

800 g calamari rings
4 spring onions (scallions), cut into 4 cm lengths
2 teaspoons peanut oil
2 limes, cut into wedges
handful picked coriander (cilantro) leaves

MARINADE
2 tablespoons plum sauce
2 tablespoons sweet chilli sauce
1 teaspoon sesame oil
1 tablespoon oyster sauce
1 tablespoon lime juice

CRUNCHY VEGETABLE SALAD
⅓ cup torn Thai basil
⅓ cup roughly chopped coriander (cilantro)
⅓ cup roughly chopped mint
2 carrots, sliced and cut into matchsticks
2 cups bean sprouts
100 g snow pea sprouts

Place all marinade ingredients in a bowl. Add calamari and spring onions, and toss to coat thoroughly. Cover bowl and refrigerate for 20 minutes.

Meanwhile, make the salad by tossing together all the ingredients in a large bowl.

Heat peanut oil in a large heavy-based frying pan or wok over very high heat. When the oil is smoking, tip in the calamari mixture and stir-fry for 5 minutes, or until cooked. Serve salad topped with calamari, with lime wedges on the side, and scattered with coriander.

1 serve = 2 units protein, 1½ units vegetables,
1 unit fats

stir-fried chilli plum calamari with crunchy vegetable salad

steamed salmon
with thai sauce

steamed salmon with thai sauce

DINNER serves 4

4 × 200 g salmon fillets
1 clove garlic, finely sliced
1 × 2 cm piece fresh ginger, finely chopped
1 stalk lemongrass, white part only, finely sliced
4 kaffir lime leaves, finely sliced
2 tablespoons fish sauce
1 teaspoon sesame oil
4 spring onions (scallions), finely sliced
4 slices lime
⅓ cup roughly chopped coriander (cilantro)
1 large red chilli, finely sliced
lime wedges

Place a bamboo steamer in a large frying pan or wok, then pour a little water into the pan. (The water level should not reach the middle of the steamer.) Bring the water to a boil.

Meanwhile, place fish on a small plate that fits into the steamer (you may need to cook the fish in 2 batches, depending on the size of the steamer). In a small bowl, mix garlic, ginger, lemongrass, lime leaves, fish sauce, sesame oil and half the spring onion. Spoon the mixture over the fish, then lay the lime slices on top. Carefully transfer the plate with the fish to the steamer and steam, covered, for 10 minutes. Remove from heat, transfer fish to serving plates and spoon over cooking juices. Garnish with coriander, chilli, lime wedges and the remaining spring onion, and serve with steamed mixed vegetables.

1 serve = 2 units protein

poached blue-eye with peperonata & basil

DINNER serves 4

3 lemons
1 litre chicken stock or fish stock
2 sprigs flat-leaf (Italian) parsley
5 black peppercorns
1 bay leaf
4 × 200 g fillets blue-eye trevalla

PEPERONATA
2 tablespoons olive oil
2 red capsicums (peppers), seeded and sliced
1 red (Spanish) onion, finely chopped
2 cloves garlic, finely chopped
1 cup torn basil
freshly ground black pepper

Cut 1 lemon into slices and place in a deep frying pan along with stock, parsley, peppercorns and bay leaf, and bring to a boil. Reduce heat and simmer for 3 minutes. Add fish and simmer very gently for 8 minutes. Remove pan from heat and allow fish to rest in the liquid.

Meanwhile, heat a large saucepan over medium heat. Add oil and capsicum and cook for 5 minutes, or until the capsicum starts to soften. Add onion and garlic and cook for a further 5 minutes. Stir in basil and season well with pepper. Spoon this peperonata onto serving plates and top with fish. Serve with lemon wedges and your favourite steamed greens.

1 serve = 2 units protein, 1 unit vegetables, 2 units fats

sesame ocean trout with mixed mushrooms

DINNER serves 4

3 limes, quartered
1 tablespoon black sesame seeds
2 teaspoons white sesame seeds
4 × 200 g ocean trout fillets, skin removed
1 tablespoon canola oil
1 clove garlic, crushed
1 × 2 cm piece fresh ginger, finely sliced
3 spring onions (scallions), finely sliced
400 g mixed mushrooms (oyster, shiitake, Swiss brown), large ones sliced
6 baby bok choy (pak choi), halved
2 tablespoons oyster sauce
2 tablespoons water
⅓ cup roughly chopped coriander (cilantro)

Preheat oven 200°C (390°F). Squeeze enough lime quarters to yield 2 tablespoons lime juice, and reserve the others.

In a small bowl, combine the sesame seeds. Sprinkle seeds over fish, then transfer fillets to a baking tray. Bake for 10 minutes, or until cooked – when cooked, the flesh will flake away easily when pressed with a fork.

Meanwhile, heat oil in large frying pan or wok over high heat. Add garlic, ginger and spring onions and cook for 2 minutes, or until onions are soft. Add mushrooms and bok choy and toss together. Add lime juice, oyster sauce and water and stir-fry for 2–3 minutes. Finally, toss through coriander. Place stir-fried mushrooms on plates and top with ocean trout. Serve the remaining lime wedges on the side.

1 serve = 2 units protein, 1½ units vegetables, 1 unit fats

fish stew with tomato & basil

fish stew with tomato & basil

DINNER serves 4

1 tablespoon olive oil
1 leek, white part only, finely sliced and washed
2 sticks celery, sliced
2 cloves garlic, crushed
1 bulb fennel, finely sliced
1 × 400 g tin chopped tomatoes
1 cup white wine
2 cups fish stock or chicken stock
800 g fish fillets (blue-eye, flathead or ling),
    cut into 4 cm pieces
¼ cup roughly chopped basil
finely grated zest of 1 lemon and 2 tablespoons juice

Heat oil in a heavy-based saucepan over medium heat.
Add leek, celery, garlic and fennel and cook for 10 minutes,
or until vegetables are soft. Add tomatoes, wine and stock
and bring to a boil. Reduce heat and simmer for 20 minutes.
Add fish and simmer for a further 10 minutes. Gently stir
through basil, lemon zest and lemon juice, reserving a little
basil and zest to garnish, if desired. Season to taste.

Serve with a big green salad and crusty bread from
your daily bread allowance.

1 serve = 2 units protein, 1 unit vegetables, 1 unit fats

steamed bream with lemon & capers

DINNER serves 4

1 small red (Spanish) onion, finely diced
1 tablespoon capers, chopped
2 tablespoons flat-leaf (Italian) parsley
2 tablespoons olive oil
juice and finely grated zest of 2 lemons
4 × 200 g bream fillets
300 g baby squash
150 g baby spinach

Preheat oven to 200°C (390°F).

In a small bowl, combine onion, capers, parsley,
1 tablespoon of the oil and half the lemon juice and zest.

Tear off 4 large pieces of foil. Place a fish fillet in the
centre of each and spoon over lemon and caper mixture.
Bring together the long sides of each foil parcel and fold
the edge over several times. Now fold in the short ends
of the foil several times to ensure the parcel is well sealed.
Transfer parcels to a baking tray and cook for 10 minutes,
or until fish is cooked through. (The exact cooking time will
depend on the thickness of the fillets.)

Meanwhile, steam squash for 5 minutes, or until
cooked. Drain and slice thickly while still hot. Transfer
to a large bowl and add spinach leaves. Toss to combine,
and drizzle with remaining lemon juice and zest. Season
lightly and serve alongside the steamed bream.

1 serve = 2 units protein, 1½ units vegetables,
2 units fats

Most flavours go very well with chicken and pork, so try the following simple recipes, and then don't be afraid to experiment by adding your own favourite herbs and spices.

chicken & pork

chicken tortillas with roasted corn salsa

LUNCH serves 4

⅓ cup low-fat sour cream
4 large wholemeal tortillas
1 iceberg lettuce, shredded
2 tomatoes, diced
400 g cooked skinless chicken breast, finely sliced

CORN SALSA
2 corn cobs
1 tablespoon olive oil
⅓ cup roughly chopped coriander (cilantro)
¼ cup roughly chopped mint
½ small red (Spanish) onion, finely diced
juice of 1 lime

To make corn salsa, preheat grill plate or barbecue grill to high. Lightly brush corn with half the oil, then grill, turning occasionally, for 10 minutes, or until lightly browned all over. Remove from the grill and allow to cool. Cut kernels from cobs and transfer kernels to a small bowl. Add remaining oil plus coriander, mint, onion and lime juice, and toss to combine.

To serve, spread 1 tablespoon of sour cream down the centre of each tortilla. Top sour cream with a small handful of lettuce, some chopped tomato and a quarter of the sliced chicken, leaving a little room at the top and bottom of the tortilla. Spoon a quarter of the corn salsa on top. Fold up bottom of tortilla, then wrap each side over the tortilla. You should have a neat, tight wrap. Repeat with the remaining tortillas and serve immediately.

1 serve = 1 unit protein, 2 units bread,
1½ units vegetables, 1 unit fats

marinated chicken rice paper rolls

LUNCH serves 4 (makes 8 rolls)

400 g skinless chicken breast fillets
8 sheets rice paper
1 cup bean sprouts
16 mint leaves
¼ cup loosely packed coriander (cilantro) leaves
½ red capsicum (pepper), seeded and sliced
1 carrot, cut into sticks

MARINADE
2 tablespoons Char Siu Sauce
    (Chinese barbecue sauce)
1 teaspoon Chinese five-spice powder
2 teaspoons freshly grated ginger
1 teaspoon rice-wine vinegar

Preheat oven to 180°C (350°F).

Mix marinade ingredients together in a bowl. Add chicken and toss to coat thoroughly. Cover bowl and allow the chicken to marinate for 10–15 minutes.

Transfer chicken to a baking dish and cook for 15 minutes, or until cooked through. Remove from the oven and allow to cool. Slice chicken into long strips and set aside.

Fill a large, shallow bowl with cold water. One by one, soak sheets of rice paper in cold water for 2 minutes, then drain and lay on a clean cloth. Divide chicken and remaining ingredients equally among the centres of the rice paper sheets. Tuck in both sides and roll up securely.

Serve with a sweet-chilli dipping sauce and a mixed-leaf salad.

1 serve = 1 unit protein, 1 unit bread,
½ unit vegetables

marinated chicken rice paper rolls

chicken, tomato & zucchini pizza

chicken, tomato & zucchini pizza

LUNCH serves 4

4 small wholemeal pita breads
⅓ cup tomato paste
2 teaspoons dried Greek oregano
2 ripe tomatoes, thinly sliced
2 zucchini (courgettes), thinly sliced lengthways
400 g cooked skinless chicken breast, sliced
100 g feta or mozzarella
1⅓ cups rocket (arugula)
1 tablespoon olive oil

Preheat oven to 200°C (390°F).

Spread pita breads with tomato paste and sprinkle with oregano. Divide tomato and zucchini between pitas, add a layer of sliced chicken and crumble feta or mozzarella over the top. Bake for 10 minutes.

Serve topped with rocket leaves and a drizzle of olive oil and with a salad alongside.

1 serve = 1 unit protein, 2 units bread, 1 unit dairy, ½ unit vegetables, 1 unit fats

pita bread pizzas

Pizzas are a delicious way to use up leftovers. Keep a packet of pita breads in the freezer for emergency meals, and use any toppings you like.

chicken caesar salad

LUNCH serves 4

4 slices wholegrain bread
1 cos lettuce, outer leaves discarded, leaves separated
250 g cooked skinless chicken breast
2 slices lean bacon, grilled and roughly chopped
2 eggs, hard-boiled and roughly chopped
50 g parmesan, coarsely grated
oil-free Caesar dressing

Lightly toast bread, then cut into 2 cm squares to make croutons and set aside.

Divide cos leaves among 4 serving plates. Cut chicken into thick slices and place on top. Sprinkle with bacon, egg, croutons and parmesan. Drizzle with dressing and serve immediately.

1 serve = 1 unit protein, 1 unit bread, ½ unit dairy, 1 unit vegetables

baked chicken breast stuffed with parsley, lemon & pine nuts

DINNER serves 4

2 spring onions (scallions), finely sliced
200 g low-fat ricotta
finely grated zest of 1 lemon
¼ cup chopped flat-leaf (Italian) parsley
1 tablespoon lemon juice
¼ cup pine nuts, lightly toasted
4 × 180 g skinless chicken breast fillets
8 thin slices prosciutto
1 tablespoon olive oil

In a small bowl, combine the spring onions, ricotta, lemon zest and juice, parsley and pine nuts. Season lightly, then cover and refrigerate for 10 minutes.

Meanwhile, with a sharp knife, make a long incision along the side and into the centre of each chicken breast, being careful not to cut through to the other side.

Spoon a quarter of the ricotta mixture into each breast. Place 2 slices of prosciutto on your work surface, overlapping them slightly. Place a stuffed chicken breast across the prosciutto, then roll up and secure with toothpicks. Repeat with remaining chicken and prosciutto.

Preheat oven to 180°C (350°F).

Heat oil in a frying pan over high heat. Add chicken and cook for 4 minutes each side, then transfer to a baking tray. Bake for 10 minutes, or until cooked through.

Serve chicken with mixed steamed vegetables.

1 serve = 2 units protein, 1 unit dairy, 3 units fats

lemon & chilli chicken skewers

LUNCH serves 4

1 clove garlic, crushed
¼ cup lemon juice
1 green chilli, seeded and finely chopped
½ cup buttermilk
400 g skinless chicken breast, cut into 2 cm cubes

In a large bowl, combine garlic, lemon juice, chilli and buttermilk. Add chicken and turn to coat thoroughly. Cover bowl and allow chicken to marinate for 30 minutes.

If using bamboo skewers, soak them in hot water for 30 minutes before use.

Preheat a grill plate or barbecue grill to high.

Thread chicken pieces onto 8 skewers. Grill for 2 minutes each side – 8 minutes in total – or until cooked through.

Serve skewers with a large helping of your favourite salad or steamed vegetables.

1 serve = 1 unit protein

lemon & chilli chicken skewers

roasted chicken with thyme, red onions & butternut pumpkin

DINNER serves 4

finely grated zest and juice of 1 lemon
1 clove garlic, roughly chopped
1 tablespoon picked lemon thyme leaves
¼ cup chopped flat-leaf (Italian) parsley
2 tablespoons olive oil
1.5 kg skinless chicken drumsticks and
    thighs on the bone, trimmed of fat
4 red (Spanish) onions, peeled and halved
600 g butternut pumpkin, peeled and
    cut into 4 cm pieces

Preheat oven to 180°C (350°F).

Place lemon zest, lemon juice, garlic, thyme, parsley and half the oil in a food processor and blend until smooth. Grease a large ovenproof baking dish with the remaining oil, arrange chicken pieces in the dish and spoon on herb mixture. Rub mixture into chicken pieces and season lightly. Add onions and pumpkin to dish and cover with foil. Roast for 20 minutes. Remove foil, baste chicken with cooking juices, and bake for a further 40 minutes.

Serve with steamed greens or a salad.

1 serve = 2 units protein, 1½ units vegetables, 2 units fats

marinated chicken with steamed greens

DINNER serves 4

2 cloves garlic, crushed
2 teaspoons freshly grated ginger
2 spring onions (scallions), sliced
1 tablespoon chopped coriander (cilantro) stalks
¼ cup light coconut milk
2 tablespoons fish sauce
2 teaspoons dry sherry (or Chinese rice wine)
1 tablespoon dark soy sauce
2 teaspoons sesame oil
1 large red chilli, finely sliced
800 g skinless chicken thigh fillets,
    trimmed of fat
4 baby bok choy (pak choi)
handful roughly chopped coriander (cilantro) leaves

Place garlic, ginger, spring onions, coriander stalks and coconut milk in a food processor and blend to form a paste. Transfer paste to a large bowl and add fish sauce, sherry, soy sauce, sesame oil and chilli, stirring to combine. Add chicken and toss to coat thoroughly. Cover and refrigerate for 1 hour.

Preheat oven to 200°C (390°F).

Transfer chicken pieces to a rack placed in a baking dish and bake for 35 minutes. Remove chicken from oven, cover with foil and set aside to rest for 5 minutes.

Meanwhile, steam bok choy and divide among serving plates. Add chicken, sprinkle with extra coriander and serve with extra steamed greens, such as choy sum, and rice or noodles from your daily bread allowance, if desired.

1 serve = 2 units protein, 1 unit vegetables, 1 unit fats

marinated chicken with steamed greens

chargrilled pesto chicken with tabouleh

chargrilled pesto chicken with tabouleh

DINNER serves 4

4 × 200 g skinless chicken breast fillets
1 lemon, cut into wedges

PESTO
(or use bought pesto)
1 cup loosely packed basil leaves
1 clove garlic, crushed
1 tablespoon lemon juice
1 tablespoon olive oil
1 tablespoon pine nuts

TABOULEH
1 cup burghul (cracked wheat)
2 cups boiling water
4 spring onions (scallions), finely sliced
12 cherry tomatoes, halved
2 tablespoons chopped mint
juice of 1 lemon
2 tablespoons olive oil
½ cup roughly chopped flat-leaf (Italian) parsley

Place pesto ingredients in a food processor and blend to a coarse paste. Rub pesto into chicken. Preheat a grill plate or barbecue grill to high. Cook chicken for 6 minutes each side, or until cooked through.

Meanwhile, place burghul in a heatproof bowl, pour boiling water over and leave for 15 minutes. Fluff with a fork, then add remaining tabouleh ingredients and stir to combine.

Slice chicken and serve with tabouleh and lemon wedges and a side salad.

1 serve = 2 units protein, 2 units bread,
½ unit vegetables, 3 units fats

chicken & leek pie

LUNCH serves 4

1 tablespoon olive oil
400 g skinless chicken thigh fillets, trimmed of fat,
    cut into 4 cm pieces
2 sticks celery, sliced
2 leeks, white part only, sliced and washed
1 cup chicken stock
1 tablespoon cornflour (cornstarch) mixed
    with ½ cup white wine
1 tablespoon chopped tarragon
1 tablespoon chopped flat-leaf (Italian) parsley
½ cup frozen peas
1 quantity olive oil pastry (see page 209)
low-fat milk, for brushing

Heat oil in a large heavy-based saucepan over medium heat. Add chicken in batches and cook for 5 minutes, or until browned. Return all chicken pieces to pan, add celery and leek and cook for 5 minutes, or until leek is soft. Pour in chicken stock and cornflour mixture and bring to a boil. Reduce heat, cover and simmer for 20 minutes. Stir in herbs and peas and season lightly. Spoon chicken filling into a 2 litre ovenproof pie dish and set aside to cool slightly.

Preheat oven to 200°C (390°F).

Roll out pastry to 5 mm thickness and the size of the pie dish. Brush rim of dish with a little milk, then drape pastry over, pressing edges firmly onto the rim of the dish. Brush pastry lid with a little more milk and bake for 20 minutes. Serve with your favourite green vegetables.

1 serve = 1 unit protein, 1 unit bread,
1 unit vegetables, 3 units fats

coq au vin

2 tablespoons olive oil
100 g lean bacon, sliced
350 g small brown onions, peeled
1 clove garlic, crushed
900 g skinless chicken drumsticks and
    thighs on the bone, trimmed of fat
2 cups red wine
1 cup chicken stock
3 Roma (plum) tomatoes, diced
2 bay leaves
1 tablespoon cornflour (cornstarch) mixed
    with 2 tablespoons cold water
250 g button mushrooms
200 g green beans, trimmed
2 tablespoons chopped flat-leaf (Italian) parsley

Heat half the oil in a large heavy-based saucepan over high heat. Add bacon, onion and garlic and cook for 5 minutes, or until onion is soft. Remove from pan and set aside. Return pan to heat, add remaining oil and cook chicken in batches for 5 minutes, or until golden. Return all chicken and bacon mixture to pan, add wine, stock, tomatoes and bay leaves and bring to a boil. Reduce heat and simmer, covered, for 45 minutes, or until chicken is tender. Remove lid, stir in cornflour mixture and mushrooms and simmer, uncovered, for a further 10 minutes.

Meanwhile, steam beans in a steamer for 5 minutes. Serve coq au vin sprinkled with parsley and with beans on the side.

1 serve = 2 units protein, 1½ units vegetables, 2 units fats

pork & onion kebabs

400 g pork fillet, cut into 2 cm cubes
2 small red (Spanish) onions, cut into wedges

MARINADE
2 tablespoons finely chopped thyme
finely grated zest and juice of 1 orange
2 tablespoons olive oil
1 tablespoon honey
1 tablespoon lemon juice
1 clove garlic, roughly chopped

Place all marinade ingredients in a large bowl. Add pork and, using a wooden spoon, turn to coat thoroughly. Cover bowl and refrigerate for 1–2 hours.

If using bamboo skewers, soak them in hot water for 30 minutes before use.

Preheat a grill plate or barbecue grill to high.

Thread pork and onion onto 4 long skewers. Grill for 2 minutes each side – 8 minutes in total – or until cooked through. Serve with a mixed-leaf salad.

1 serve = 1 unit protein, 2 units fats

pork & onion kebabs

pork loin with tomato & sage

DINNER serves 4

1 × 800 g pork loin
16 sage leaves
1 tablespoon olive oil
2 tablespoons lemon juice
3 large ripe tomatoes, cut into 1 cm dice
½ cup white wine
200 g broccolini
200 g carrots
2 tablespoons flat-leaf (Italian) parsley leaves

Cut pork loin into 8 steaks. Place steaks, cut-side up, on
a chopping board and cover with plastic wrap. Using
a rolling pin, lightly flatten to 5 mm thickness. Remove
plastic wrap and place 4 sage leaves on half of the steaks,
then top with the remaining steaks. Secure with a toothpick
at either end.

Heat oil in a heavy-based frying pan over medium
heat. Add pork and cook for 5 minutes each side, or until
browned. Remove from pan, cover lightly with foil and set
aside to rest.

Return pan to heat, add lemon juice, tomatoes and
wine and bring to a boil. Reduce heat and simmer for
2 minutes. Return pork to pan and continue to simmer
for 8 minutes.

Meanwhile, steam broccolini and carrots. Divide
vegetables among serving plates and arrange pork
alongside. Sprinkle pork with parsley and serve
immediately.

1 serve = 2 units protein, 1½ units vegetables,
1 unit fats

pork cutlet with avocado, orange & beetroot salad

DINNER serves 4

2 tablespoons redcurrant jelly or cranberry sauce
4 × 200 g pork cutlets, trimmed of fat

AVOCADO, ORANGE & BEETROOT SALAD
1 avocado, thickly sliced
2 oranges, segmented
700 g tinned baby beetroots, drained and halved
100 g rocket (arugula)
¼ cup roughly chopped mint
½ red (Spanish) onion, finely sliced
1 tablespoon olive oil
2 teaspoons lemon juice

Preheat a grill plate or barbecue grill to high. Rub
redcurrant jelly into the pork using your fingers, then transfer
immediately to the grill plate and cook for 4 minutes each
side, or until browned and cooked through. Set aside for
5 minutes.

Place avocado, orange, beetroot, rocket, mint and onion
in a bowl and toss lightly. Drizzle with oil and lemon juice.

Serve pork cutlets with salad alongside.

1 serve = 2 units protein, ½ unit fruit,
1 unit vegetables, 1 unit fats

pork cutlet with avocado, orange & beetroot salad

This chapter and the next contain more delicious recipe ideas for the important red-meat component of the CSIRO Total Wellbeing Diet. Cheaper cuts of meat can often be substituted, so don't be afraid to tell your butcher how you will be cooking the meat, and to ask if there are suitable alternative cuts.

beef & veal

beef kebabs with currant couscous & harissa

DINNER serves 4

2 red (Spanish) onions, quartered
1 yellow capsicum (pepper), cut into 2 cm dice
2 small zucchini (courgettes), halved lengthways
    and then cut into 2 cm pieces
800 g beef rump, cut into cubes
1 tablespoon lemon juice
1 tablespoon olive oil
¾ cup couscous (makes 1⅓ cups
    cooked couscous)
¼ cup currants
1½ cups boiling water
2 teaspoons extra-virgin olive oil
1 lemon, cut into wedges

HARISSA
(makes approx 2 cups; store leftovers in the fridge)
1 teaspoon ground coriander
1 teaspoon ground cumin
½ teaspoon ground fennel
½ teaspoon ground cinnamon
4 roasted red capsicums (peppers), chopped
    (to roast your own capsicums, see page 190)
¼ cup roughly chopped mint
2 cloves garlic, roughly chopped
1 small red chilli, chopped
finely grated zest and juice of 1 lime
2 tablespoons olive oil

To make the harissa, place all ingredients in a food processor and blend until smooth. Set aside.

If using bamboo skewers, soak in hot water for 30 minutes before use. Preheat a grill plate or barbecue grill to high. Thread vegetables and beef alternately onto 8 skewers. Drizzle with lemon juice and olive oil. Cook kebabs for 2 minutes each side – 8 minutes in total – or until meat is cooked and vegetables are browned. Set aside for 5 minutes.

Meanwhile, place couscous and currants in a heatproof bowl. Pour over boiling water and extra-virgin olive oil, cover with plastic wrap and allow to sit for 5 minutes. Fluff up with a fork.

Divide couscous and skewers among plates and serve with 2 tablespoons of harissa per person and a lemon wedge or two.

1 serve = 2 units protein, 1 unit bread, 1 unit vegetables, 2 units fats

sichuan pepper sirloin with broccoli & capsicum

DINNER serves 4

4 × 200 g sirloins, trimmed of fat
2 tablespoons Sichuan pepper, crushed
1 tablespoon vegetable oil
2 teaspoons sesame oil
1 small onion, sliced
1 clove garlic, finely chopped
400 g broccoli, cut into small florets
1 red capsicum (pepper), seeded and cut into strips
2 tablespoons soy sauce
1 tablespoon hoisin sauce
2 tablespoons water

Place sirloins on a large plate and sprinkle both sides of the meat with Sichuan pepper. Preheat a grill plate or barbecue grill to high and cook steaks for 4 minutes each side (for medium–rare), or until done to your liking. Transfer to a clean plate, lightly cover with foil and allow to rest for 5–10 minutes.

Meanwhile, heat a wok or large non-stick frying pan over high heat. Add oils and, when smoking, add onion and garlic and stir-fry for 2 minutes. Add broccoli and capsicum and cook for a further 2 minutes, stirring constantly. Add soy sauce, hoisin sauce and water and toss to coat. Serve vegetables alongside the peppered sirloins.

1 serve = 2 units protein, 1 unit vegetables, 1½ units fats

soy & ginger beef with broccolini

DINNER serves 4

1 litre water
1 litre salt-reduced beef stock
⅓ cup light soy sauce
2 cloves garlic, sliced
1 × 4 cm piece fresh ginger, sliced
juice of 1 lime
1 bunch coriander (cilantro),
    stalks and leaves separated
800 g lean beef fillet
2 bunches broccolini, trimmed
4 spring onions (scallions), sliced on an angle

Bring water, stock, soy sauce, garlic, ginger, lime juice and coriander stalks to a boil in a large heavy-based saucepan. Reduce heat and simmer for 10 minutes. Add beef and cook for 20 minutes. Remove beef and set aside for 10 minutes.

Meanwhile, strain stock and transfer to a clean saucepan. Return to a boil, then add broccolini and simmer for 3 minutes. Turn off the heat, add the spring onions and allow to infuse for 1 minute. Finely slice the meat.

Strain the vegetables, reserving the stock, and transfer to serving bowls. Add sliced beef and a little of the stock. To serve, scatter with coriander leaves and offer extra steamed greens.

1 serve = 2 units protein, 1 unit vegetables

soy & ginger beef with broccolini

barbecued steak with
artichoke & herb salad

barbecued steak with artichoke & herb salad

DINNER serves 4

1 tablespoon chopped rosemary
1 clove garlic, crushed
1 tablespoon olive oil
4 × 200 g rump steaks, trimmed of fat

ARTICHOKE & HERB SALAD

1 × 340 g jar marinated artichoke hearts, drained
1 tablespoon lemon juice
1 tablespoon olive oil
½ cup coarsely grated parmesan
¼ cup chopped basil
2 tablespoons chopped flat-leaf (Italian) parsley
2 cups salad leaves
freshly ground black pepper, to taste

Preheat a grill plate or barbecue grill to high.

In a small bowl, mix rosemary, garlic and olive oil. Rub into steaks using your fingers. Cook steaks for 4 minutes each side, or until done to your liking. Remove from heat, cover with foil and set aside to rest for 5–10 minutes.

To make the salad, mix all ingredients. Serve steak with salad and your favourite steamed vegetables.

1 serve = 2 units protein, 1 unit vegetables, 1 unit fats

steak & mushroom pie

LUNCH serves 4

1 tablespoon olive oil
400 g rump steak, cut into cubes
1 onion, chopped
2 cloves garlic, crushed
350 g large flat mushrooms, sliced
2 teaspoons dried mixed herbs
1 × 400 g tin diced tomatoes
1 cup salt-reduced beef stock
1 tablespoon cornflour (cornstarch) mixed
    with 2 tablespoons cold water
1 quantity olive oil pastry (see page 209)
low-fat milk, for brushing

Heat oil in a large saucepan over medium heat. Add beef in batches and cook for 5 minutes, or until browned. Return all meat to pan, add onion and garlic and cook for 3 minutes, or until onion is soft. Add mushrooms, dried herbs, tomatoes and stock and bring to a boil. Reduce heat and simmer, covered, for 30 minutes. Pour in cornflour mixture and simmer, uncovered, for a further 10 minutes, or until thick. Spoon pie filling into a 2 litre ovenproof pie dish and set aside to cool slightly.

Preheat oven to 200°C (390°F).

Roll out pastry to 5 mm thickness and the size of the pie dish. Brush rim of pie dish with a little milk, then drape pastry over, pressing the edges firmly onto the rim of the dish. Brush pastry with a little more milk and bake for 20 minutes. Serve with steamed green vegetables or a crisp green salad.

1 serve = 1 unit protein, 1 unit bread,
1 unit vegetables, 3 units fats

beef & vegetable pasta bake

2 tablespoons olive oil
800 g lean minced (ground) beef
1 red (Spanish) onion, diced
2 teaspoons dried mixed herbs
1 red capsicum (pepper), seeded and finely diced
1 × 400 g tin chopped tomatoes
1 cup salt-reduced beef stock
250 g rigatoni, cooked
2 zucchini (courgettes), diced
1 cup frozen peas
100 g grated low-fat cheddar cheese

Heat half the oil in a large heavy-based saucepan over high heat. Add mince in two batches and cook for 5 minutes, or until just browned. Transfer to a large bowl. Add remaining oil to pan, along with onion, and cook for 5 minutes, or until onion is soft. Return mince to pan, add dried herbs, capsicum, tomatoes and stock and bring to a boil. Reduce heat and simmer for 35 minutes. Stir in pasta, zucchini and peas, then carefully pour into a 2 litre ovenproof dish.

Meanwhile, preheat oven to 200°C (390°F). Sprinkle cheese over pasta bake, transfer to oven and cook for 10 minutes, or until cheese is golden. Serve with a mixed-leaf salad.

1 serve = 2 units protein, 1 unit bread, ½ unit dairy, 1 unit vegetables, 2 units fats

beef & eggplant 'cannelloni'

2 tablespoons olive oil
800 g lean minced (ground) beef
1 onion, finely diced
1 clove garlic, crushed
2 tablespoons tomato paste
2 cups salt-reduced beef stock
1 × 250 g packet frozen spinach, defrosted
freshly ground black pepper
2 large eggplants (aubergines), thinly sliced lengthways
olive oil spray
700 ml tomato passata (tomato purée)
50 g grated parmesan

Heat half the oil in a large heavy-based saucepan over high heat. Add mince in two batches and cook for 5 minutes, or until just browned. Transfer to a large bowl. Add remaining oil to pan, along with onion and garlic, and cook for 10 minutes, or until golden. Return mince to pan, add tomato paste and stir well. Add stock and bring to a boil. Reduce heat and simmer for 35 minutes. Stir in spinach and season with freshly ground black pepper.

Meanwhile, preheat oven to 200°C (390°F). Lightly spray eggplant slices with oil and bake for 15 minutes, or until golden.

Lay eggplant slices on your work surface and spoon beef mixture down the centre of each. Roll up eggplant slices. You should now have 12 eggplant 'cannelloni'. Transfer to an ovenproof dish, pour over tomato passata and sprinkle with parmesan. Bake for 10 minutes.

Serve with a crisp side salad.

1 serve = 2 units protein, ½ unit dairy, 1½ units vegetables, 2 units fats

beef stroganoff

DINNER serves 4

1 tablespoon vegetable oil
800 g lean beef strips
1 large onion, finely sliced
1 clove garlic, crushed
400 g button mushrooms, sliced
¾ cup salt-reduced beef stock
1 tablespoon Worcestershire sauce
1 tablespoon cornflour (cornstarch) mixed
    with 2 tablespoons cold water
100 g low-fat natural yoghurt
¼ cup roughly chopped flat-leaf (Italian) parsley

Heat oil in a large non-stick frying pan over medium heat. Add beef strips in batches and cook for 5 minutes, or until browned. Return all meat to pan, add onion, garlic and mushrooms and cook for 10 minutes, or until vegetables are soft. Stir in stock, Worcestershire sauce and cornflour mixture and bring to a boil. Reduce heat and simmer, covered, for 10 minutes. Stir in yoghurt and parsley, and season to taste.

Serve with rice or pasta from your daily bread allowance and steamed vegetables.

1 serve = 2 units protein, 1 unit vegetables,
1 unit fats

classic roast beef

DINNER serves 4

1 tablespoon Dijon mustard
1 kg lean topside roast
freshly ground black pepper
2 tablespoons olive oil
4 small onions, peeled
500 g pumpkin, peeled and cut into large chunks
3 parsnips, peeled and cut into large chunks
2 sprigs rosemary, leaves picked
300 g green beans

Preheat oven to 180°C (350°F).
    Using your hands, rub mustard all over beef. Season with pepper. Heat oil in a flameproof baking dish over high heat. Add beef and sear on all sides. Place onions, pumpkin and parsnips in baking dish around beef and sprinkle with rosemary. Roast for 35 minutes, or until done to your liking. Transfer meat to a plate, cover lightly with foil and allow to rest for 10 minutes.
    Meanwhile, bring a small saucepan of water to a boil. Add beans and cook for 5–6 minutes, then drain.
    Slice beef and serve with roasted vegetables and beans.

1 serve = 2 units protein, 2 units vegetables,
2 units fats

beef vindaloo

DINNER serves 4

1 teaspoon chilli powder
1 teaspoon ground cumin
½ teaspoon ground white pepper
2 tablespoons freshly grated ginger
2 cloves garlic, crushed
1 teaspoon ground turmeric
1 tablespoon olive oil
2 onions, chopped
800 g lean beef, cut into 4 cm pieces

1 stick cinnamon
½ teaspoon ground cardamom
½ teaspoon ground nutmeg
2 cups cold water
1 green chilli, finely sliced
¼ cup white-wine vinegar
2 teaspoons brown sugar
¾ cup rice (makes approx
   1⅓ cups cooked rice)

Mix chilli powder, cumin, pepper, ginger, garlic and turmeric in a small bowl, and set aside.

Heat oil in a large heavy-based saucepan over medium heat. Add onions and cook for 10 minutes, or until golden. Add beef in batches and cook for 10 minutes, or until beef is lightly browned. Return all meat to the pan, add the mixed spices plus the cinnamon, cardamom and nutmeg, and cook for 2 minutes, or until fragrant. Add water (it should just cover beef) and chilli, and bring to a boil. Reduce heat and simmer for 1 hour. Stir in vinegar and sugar and cook for a further 20 minutes.

Meanwhile, cook rice for 10–15 minutes in boiling water, then drain. Serve rice and curry with minted yoghurt (see page 184) and lots of fresh steamed vegetables.

1 serve = 2 units protein, 1 unit bread, 1 unit fats

veal escalopes with fennel, spinach & olives

DINNER serves 4

800 g veal loin, cut into 8 slices
2 tablespoons plain flour
2 tablespoons olive oil
1 bulb fennel, finely sliced
1 red (Spanish) onion, finely sliced
250 g baby spinach
12 kalamata olives
3 lemons
freshly ground black pepper

Spread a large piece of plastic wrap on your work surface. Place veal slices on top and cover with a second piece of plastic wrap. Using a rolling pin, flatten slices to 5 mm thickness. Lightly dust escalopes with flour.

Heat half the oil in a large frying pan over medium heat. Cook escalopes for 2 minutes each side, or until golden.

Meanwhile, place fennel, onion, spinach leaves and olives in a large bowl. Drizzle with remaining olive oil and the juice of 1 lemon, and season with pepper. Serve salad with veal steaks and the remaining lemons cut into wedges.

1 serve = 2 units protein, 1½ units vegetables, 2 units fats

lemon cumin veal cutlets with parsnip mash & baby green beans

DINNER serves 4

finely grated zest of 1 lemon
2 teaspoons ground cumin
1 tablespoon olive oil
1 clove garlic, crushed
4 × 200 g veal cutlets
400 g baby green beans

PARSNIP MASH
6 small parsnips (700 g), peeled
    and cut into large pieces
1 tablespoon light margarine
½ cup low-fat milk

Place lemon zest, cumin, oil and garlic in a large bowl and mix well. Add the veal cutlets and turn to coat thoroughly. Cover bowl and refrigerate for 30 minutes.

Meanwhile, place parsnips in a saucepan and cover with cold water. Bring to a boil and cook for 15 minutes, or until tender. Drain and place in a food processor with margarine and milk, and blend until smooth. Season to taste.

Preheat a grill plate or barbecue grill to high. Cook cutlets for 4 minutes each side, or until done to your liking.

Bring a saucepan of water to the boil. Place beans in a steamer and cook for 5 minutes.

Serve cutlets with parsnip mash and steamed baby green beans. Baby carrots make a delicious side dish to this.

1 serve = 2 units protein, 1½ units vegetables, 1½ units fats

lemon cumin veal cutlets with
parsnip mash & baby green beans

osso bucco with lemon & parsley

osso bucco with lemon & parsley

DINNER serves 4

2 kg large veal osso bucco (200 g meat per person)
2 tablespoons canola oil
1 onion, diced
2 carrots, roughly chopped
2 sticks celery, roughly chopped
1 clove garlic, sliced
1 tablespoon tomato paste
1 cup white wine
2 sprigs rosemary
2 cups chicken stock
1 × 400 g tin chopped tomatoes
2 teaspoons cornflour (cornstarch) mixed
    with 2 tablespoons cold water
2 tablespoons roughly chopped flat-leaf (Italian) parsley
2 tablespoons finely grated lemon zest

Heat a large heavy-based saucepan over high heat. Coat veal with half the oil and cook, in batches, for 10 minutes, or until browned. Transfer to a large ovenproof casserole.

Preheat oven to 180°C (350°F).

Heat the remaining oil in a saucepan over medium heat. Add onion, carrots, celery and garlic and cook for 5 minutes, or until vegetables are soft and lightly coloured. Add tomato paste, wine, rosemary, stock, tomatoes and cornflour and stir to combine. Pour vegetables and sauce over the veal. Cover with foil and bake for 1 hour. Remove foil and bake for a further 30 minutes. Remove from the oven and sprinkle parsley and lemon zest over the osso bucco. Serve with steamed vegetables.

1 serve = 2 units protein, 1 unit vegetables,
2 units fats

veal scaloppine with caponata

DINNER serves 4

4 × 200 g veal loin steaks
2 lemons, cut into wedges

CAPONATA
1 eggplant (aubergine), diced
olive oil spray
2 tablespoons olive oil
1 clove garlic, crushed
1 red (Spanish) onion, chopped
1 red capsicum (pepper), seeded and diced
3 Roma (plum) tomatoes, chopped
½ cup roughly torn basil

Preheat oven to 200°C (390°F).

Tip eggplant onto a baking tray and lightly spray with oil. Transfer to oven and cook for 15 minutes, or until golden.

Heat half the oil in a large saucepan over high heat. Add garlic, onion and capsicum and cook for 5 minutes. Add eggplant and tomatoes and cook for a further 10 minutes. Season lightly and stir in basil.

Meanwhile, spread a large piece of plastic wrap on your work surface. Place veal steaks on top and cover with a second piece of plastic wrap. Using a rolling pin, lightly flatten steaks.

Heat remaining oil in a large non-stick frying pan over high heat. Add scaloppine and cook for 2 minutes each side, or until done to your liking. Serve with caponata and wedges of lemon, and offer a side salad.

1 serve = 2 units protein, 1 unit vegetables,
2 units fats

The following versatile meals can easily
be halved for when there are two of you,
or doubled if you are feeding family and
friends. Just make sure you also increase
the side salads and vegetables, so everyone
gets a healthy serve.

lamb

spiced lamb salad with orange, coriander & red onion

DINNER serves 4

1 teaspoon ground cumin
juice and finely grated zest of 1 lemon
1 clove garlic, crushed
2 tablespoons olive oil
800 g lamb leg steaks
2 oranges, segmented
¼ cup roughly chopped coriander (cilantro)
½ red (Spanish) onion, finely sliced
100 g low-fat feta, crumbled
250 g baby spinach

Place cumin, lemon juice and zest, garlic and half the oil in a large dish and mix well. Add lamb, turning to coat thoroughly, then cover and set aside for 10 minutes.

Meanwhile, place remaining oil in a bowl, add oranges, coriander, onion, feta and spinach leaves and toss well.

Preheat a grill plate or barbecue grill to high. Add lamb and cook for 3 minutes each side, or until done to your liking. Serve with the salad.

1 serve = 2 units protein, ½ unit dairy, ½ unit fruit, 1 unit vegetables, 2 units fats

barbecued lamb & vegetable wrap with pesto

LUNCH serves 4

400 g lamb rump steaks
2 zucchini (courgettes), thinly sliced lengthways
2 red capsicums (peppers), seeded and sliced
1 red (Spanish) onion, sliced into thick rings
2 teaspoons picked thyme leaves
1 tablespoon olive oil
4 large wholemeal Lebanese flatbreads
⅓ cup pesto
2 cups rocket (arugula)

Preheat a grill plate or barbecue grill to high. Cook lamb steaks for 4 minutes each side, or until done to your liking. Remove to a plate, cover with foil and set aside to rest for 5 minutes.

Place zucchini, capsicums, onion and thyme in a bowl. Add olive oil and toss to coat. Transfer mixture to grill plate and cook, turning occasionally, for 2–5 minutes, or until charred and soft. Set aside.

Slice lamb across the grain into thin strips. To serve, spread each flatbread with a quarter of the pesto. Top with a quarter each of the chargrilled vegetables, lamb and rocket. Fold up the bottom of the wrap, then cross the sides over each other. Repeat with remaining wraps and serve immediately.

1 serve = 1 unit protein, 2 units bread, 1½ units vegetables, 2 units fats

barbecued lamb &
vegetable wrap with pesto

lamb & rosemary sausages

DINNER serves 4

750 g lean minced (ground) lamb
1 red (Spanish) onion, finely chopped
1 tablespoon chopped rosemary
1 tablespoon chopped flat-leaf (Italian) parsley
50 g wholemeal breadcrumbs
1 egg, lightly beaten
1 tablespoon olive oil

In a large bowl, mix all ingredients except olive oil. Season lightly. Form mixture into 8 equal portions, then roll each to form a sausage shape.

Heat oil in a large heavy-based frying pan over medium heat. Add sausages and cook, turning frequently, for 10 minutes, or until all sides are golden and sausages are cooked through. Serve with a salad, greens or pumpkin mash – or all three.

1 serve = 2 units protein, 1 unit fats

lamb kofta with tomato salad

DINNER serves 4

700 g lean minced (ground) lamb
2 Weet-bix, crushed, or ⅓ cup unprocessed wheatbran
finely grated zest of 1 lemon
1 tablespoon garam masala
2 cloves garlic, crushed
2 eggs, lightly beaten
2 tablespoons vegetable oil

MINTED YOGHURT
2 cups low-fat natural yoghurt
2 tablespoons mint sauce
½ cup freshly chopped mint

TOMATO SALAD
6 ripe tomatoes, diced
2 red (Spanish) onions, finely diced
⅔ cup loosely packed coriander (cilantro)
⅔ cup loosely packed flat-leaf (Italian) parsley

If using bamboo skewers, soak them in hot water for 30 minutes before use.

In a bowl, mix lamb, Weet-bix, lemon zest, garam masala, garlic and eggs. Season lightly. Form mixture into 8 short, thick sausages. Thread onto skewers.

Heat oil a large non-stick frying pan over medium heat. Add koftas and cook for 5 minutes each side, or until cooked through.

Meanwhile, mix minted yoghurt ingredients in a small bowl. Mix all tomato salad ingredients in a separate bowl and divide among serving plates. Arrange koftas on top and serve with minted yoghurt.

1 serve = 2 units protein, ½ unit dairy,
1 unit vegetables, 2 units fats

lamb kofta with tomato salad

spicy lamb burger with tzatziki

spicy lamb burger with tzatziki

LUNCH serves 4

2 tablespoons low-fat hummus
4 slices wholegrain bread, lightly toasted
2 baby cos lettuces, outer leaves discarded,
    leaves separated
2 ripe tomatoes, sliced

BURGER PATTIES
400 g lean minced (ground) lamb
1 red (Spanish) onion, finely diced
1 small red chilli, seeded and finely chopped
½ cup roughly chopped coriander (cilantro)
1 clove garlic, crushed
2 teaspoons freshly grated ginger

TZATZIKI
½ cup low-fat natural yoghurt
1 Lebanese cucumber, seeded and finely diced
⅓ cup roughly chopped mint

In a large bowl, mix all patty ingredients thoroughly.
Form mixture into 4 patties.

Preheat a grill plate or barbecue grill to high.
Add patties and cook for 8 minutes each side,
or until cooked through. Meanwhile, in a small bowl,
mix yoghurt, cucumber and mint.

To serve, spread a quarter of the hummus on
each slice of bread. Layer with cos leaves, tomato
and a burger patty, and top with a dollop of tatziki.

1 serve = 1 unit protein, 1 unit bread,
1 unit vegetables

lunchboxes
A versatile lunch or dinner meal, burgers freeze extremely
well. Make double the recipe and freeze for later use.

indian lamb patties

DINNER serves 4

750 g lean minced (ground) lamb
1 small onion, finely chopped
1 clove garlic, finely chopped
1 tablespoon garam masala
½ cup roughly chopped coriander (cilantro)
¼ cup roughly chopped mint
1 tablespoon spicy mango chutney
1 egg, lightly beaten
1 cup low-fat natural yoghurt

Place all ingredients except yoghurt in a large bowl
and mix well. Season lightly. Form mixture into 8 patties.
Transfer to a plate, cover and refrigerate for 15 minutes.

Heat a grill plate or barbecue grill to high. Add patties
and cook for 6–8 minutes each side, or until cooked
through. Serve with a dollop of yoghurt and steamed
green vegetables or a salad.

1 serve = 2 units protein

lamb loin chops with asian coleslaw

DINNER serves 4

950 g lamb loin chops (200 g meat per person)
2 tablespoons plum sauce
2 cups shredded Chinese cabbage
1 cup bean sprouts
½ red capsicum (pepper), seeded and finely sliced
4 spring onions (scallions), finely sliced
1 carrot, coarsely grated
¼ cup shredded mint
¼ cup roughly chopped coriander (cilantro)
¼ cup soy sauce
2 tablespoons lime juice
1 tablespoon fish sauce
2 tablespoons sweet chilli sauce

Preheat a grill plate or barbecue grill to high. Brush chops with plum sauce, then cook, being careful not to burn the sauce, for 5 minutes each side, or until done to your liking.

Meanwhile, place remaining ingredients in a bowl and mix well. Cover bowl and set aside for 5 minutes to allow the flavours to infuse. Serve with the chops.

1 serve = 2 units protein, 1 unit vegetables

polenta-crumbed lamb chops with zucchini & feta

DINNER serves 4

1 egg, lightly beaten
¼ cup wholemeal plain flour
¼ cup polenta
2 tablespoons finely chopped flat-leaf (Italian) parsley
800 g lamb chops
olive oil spray
1 tablespoon olive oil
2 zucchini (courgettes), diced
3 tomatoes, diced
1 red (Spanish) onion, diced
⅓ cup shredded basil
50 g feta, crumbled into small pieces

Preheat a grill plate or barbecue grill to high. Pour egg onto a large dinner plate. Scatter flour over a second dinner plate. Combine polenta and parsley on a third dinner plate.

Crumb chops by coating them with flour, then dipping them in beaten egg, then coating them with the polenta and parsley mixture. Spray chops lightly with oil and grill for 5 minutes each side, or until golden.

Meanwhile, heat oil in a large non-stick frying pan over high heat. Add zucchini, tomatoes and onion and cook for 2 minutes. Stir in basil and feta, and season to taste. Serve with the chops.

1 serve = 2 units protein, ½ unit dairy, 1 unit vegetables, 1 unit fats

italian lamb meatloaf

700 g lean minced (ground) lamb
1 onion, finely diced
2 cloves garlic, finely chopped
1 teaspoon dried mixed herbs
3 Roma (plum) tomatoes, finely diced
2 tablespoons tomato sauce (ketchup)
¼ cup roughly chopped flat-leaf (Italian) parsley
70 g wholemeal breadcrumbs
2 eggs, lightly beaten
1 × 250 g packet frozen spinach, defrosted
¼ cup pine nuts, lightly toasted

Preheat oven to 180°C (350°F). Lightly grease a loaf tin.
   In a large bowl, mix all ingredients using your hands. Season lightly. Press mixture into loaf tin, cover with foil and bake for 40 minutes. Remove foil and bake for a further 15 minutes, or until a brown crust forms. Tilt loaf tin and drain off any excess liquid, then allow meatloaf to stand for 10 minutes before cutting and serving.

1 serve = 2 units protein, ½ unit bread,
1 unit vegetables, 1½ units fats

lamb saag

2 tablespoons vegetable oil
2 onions, sliced
2 cardamom pods, lightly crushed
1 stick cinnamon
1 tablespoon garam masala
2 cloves garlic, crushed
800 g lamb leg, cut into 3 cm cubes
2 tablespoons water, plus 1 cup extra water
1 green chilli, finely chopped
2 Roma (plum) tomatoes, diced
1 × 500 g packet frozen spinach, defrosted
⅔ cup low-fat natural yoghurt

Heat oil in a large heavy-based saucepan over high heat. Add onions, cardamom pods and cinnamon and cook for 10 minutes, or until onions are soft and golden. Add garam masala, garlic, lamb and 2 tablespoons of water and cook for 10 minutes, or until lamb is browned and spices are fragrant. Reduce heat and add chilli, tomatoes, spinach, extra 1 cup of water and half the yoghurt, and simmer for 30–40 minutes, or until lamb is tender.
   Serve with an extra dollop of yoghurt, plus rice from your daily bread allowance.

1 serve = 2 units protein, 1 unit vegetables,
2 units fats

chermoula lamb fillet with avocado & coriander salsa

DINNER serves 4

800 g lamb fillets

CHERMOULA PASTE
1 teaspoon freshly ground black pepper
2 teaspoons ground cumin
2 teaspoons ground coriander
1 teaspoon cayenne pepper
¼ cup loosely packed flat-leaf (Italian) parsley leaves
¼ cup loosely packed coriander (cilantro) leaves
¼ cup loosely packed mint leaves
2 tablespoons lemon juice
2 spring onions (scallions), roughly chopped
1 clove garlic, roughly chopped

SALSA
1 avocado, diced
½ cup roughly chopped coriander (cilantro)
2 large tomatoes, diced
4 spring onions (scallions), finely sliced
1 roasted red capsicum (pepper), chopped
   (to roast your own capsicums, see below)
1 tablespoon lemon juice
1 tablespoon olive oil

Process all paste ingredients finely. Rub paste into lamb fillets using your fingers, and set aside
for 5 minutes. Meanwhile, preheat a grill plate or barbecue grill to high. Cook lamb for 3 minutes
each side, or as liked. Put on a plate, cover with foil and set aside for 5 minutes.

   Lightly toss all salsa ingredients, and season lightly to taste. Serve lamb fillet on salsa,
with a mixed-leaf salad or your favourite greens.

1 serve = 2 units protein, 1 unit vegetables, 2 units fats

roasting capsicums
Preheat oven to 180°C (350°F). Halve and seed capsicums and place, skin-side up,
in a baking dish. Drizzle with a little olive oil and roast for 20 minutes. Remove from oven,
cover with foil and allow to cool slightly. Peel off and discard skin.

lamb biryani

lamb biryani

DINNER serves 4

800 g lamb leg steaks, cut into 2 cm cubes
2 tablespoons vegetable oil
2 onions, finely sliced
2 cloves garlic, crushed
1 tablespoon finely chopped fresh ginger
1 green chilli, seeded and finely chopped
2 teaspoons garam masala
1 teaspoon ground turmeric
1 teaspoon ground cinnamon
½ teaspoon ground cardamom
½ teaspoon ground nutmeg
½ teaspoon cayenne pepper
1 bay leaf
½ cup low-fat natural yoghurt
¼ cup lime juice
½ cup basmati rice
¼ cup sultanas
handful roughly chopped coriander (cilantro)
2 tablespoons roughly chopped toasted cashews

Heat a large heavy-based saucepan over high heat. Coat lamb in half the oil and cook, in batches, for 5 minutes, or until browned. Remove from pan.

Heat remaining oil in pan. Cook onions and garlic for 6 minutes. Add ginger, chilli, spices and bay leaf and cook for 2 minutes more. Stir through yoghurt and lime juice. Mix in lamb, then cover and simmer for 10 minutes. Mix in rice and ¾ cup water. Preheat oven to 180°C (350°F).

Transfer to an ovenproof dish and cover with foil. Bake for 30–40 minutes, or until rice is cooked. Set aside for 5 minutes. Stir through sultanas, garnish with coriander and cashews and serve with a green salad.

1 serve = 2 units protein, 1 unit bread, ½ unit fruit, 3 units fats

moussaka

DINNER serves 4

2 tablespoons olive oil
800 g lean minced (ground) lamb
1 large onion, diced
2 cloves garlic, crushed
2 teaspoons ground cinnamon
1 × 400 g tin chopped tomatoes
2 tablespoons roughly chopped oregano
1 cup salt-reduced chicken stock
4 eggplants (aubergines)
olive oil spray
100 g low-fat ricotta
¼ cup low-fat milk
100 g grated low-fat cheddar

Preheat oven to 200°C (390°F).

Heat oil in a large heavy-based saucepan over high heat. Cook lamb, in two batches, for 5 minutes, or until browned. Remove from pan and set aside. Heat remaining oil in pan. Add onion, garlic and cinnamon and cook for 5 minutes, or until onion is soft. Return meat to pan, add tomatoes, oregano and stock and bring to a boil. Reduce heat and simmer for 25 minutes.

Meanwhile, slice eggplants lengthways and spray both sides lightly with oil. Bake for 10 minutes, or until golden.

Spoon a quarter of the mince into a 2 litre baking dish, in an even layer. Cover with a third of the eggplant slices. Repeat layers, finishing with mince.

In a small bowl, mix ricotta, milk and cheese. Spoon over top of moussaka and bake for 30 minutes, or until golden brown. Serve with a crisp green salad.

1 serve = 2 units protein, 1 unit dairy, 1½ units vegetables, 2 units fats

lamb tagine

DINNER serves 4

1 onion, roughly chopped
2 cloves garlic, roughly chopped
½ cup roughly chopped flat-leaf (Italian) parsley
½ cup roughly chopped coriander (cilantro)
1 green chilli, roughly chopped
2 teaspoons ground cinnamon
¼ cup pitted dates, roughly chopped
2 teaspoons finely grated lemon zest
800 g lean lamb shoulder, trimmed of fat
 and cut into 2 cm pieces

1 tablespoon vegetable oil
1 cup water
1 × 400 g tin chopped tomatoes
¾ cup couscous (makes 1⅓ cups
 cooked couscous)
1 cup boiling water
1 teaspoon olive oil
100 g low-fat natural yoghurt

Blend onion, garlic, parsley, coriander, chilli, cinnamon, dates and lemon zest in
a food processor until smooth. Set aside.

Heat a large heavy-based saucepan over high heat. Coat lamb with oil and cook,
in small batches, for 5 minutes, or until browned. Return all lamb pieces to pan, add paste
and stir to coat. Cook for 3–5 minutes, until aromatic. Add water and tomatoes and mix well.
Bring to a boil, then reduce heat and simmer, covered, for 1½ hours, stirring occasionally.
Season lightly.

Meanwhile, place couscous in a bowl and pour over boiling water and olive oil. Cover
with plastic wrap and allow to sit for 5 minutes, or until water is absorbed. Fluff up with a fork.

Serve tagine with couscous, a dollop of yoghurt and lots of steamed vegetables.

1 serve = 2 units protein, 1 unit bread, 1 unit vegetables, 1 unit fats

The following pages contain several ideas
for side serves of vegetables, but this is just
the tip of the iceberg. Cook these recipes,
then use them as a base from which to
create your own delicious and healthy sides.

vegetables

zucchini with spinach & goat's cheese

SIDES serves 4

3 zucchini (courgettes), finely sliced into rounds
150 g baby spinach
2 teaspoons finely grated lemon zest
1 tablespoon olive oil
50 g goat's cheese, crumbled
¼ cup torn basil

Bring a large saucepan of lightly salted water to a boil.
Add zucchini and cook for 3 minutes. Drain zucchini
in a colander and return to saucepan over low heat.
Add spinach, lemon zest and olive oil and stir until
spinach has wilted. Add goat's cheese and basil
and season lightly.

　　Goes well with lamb or chicken.

1 serve = ½ unit dairy, 1 unit vegetables, 1 unit fats

white beans with spring onions & fresh herbs

SIDES serves 4

1 tablespoon olive oil
4 spring onions (scallions), finely sliced
1 clove garlic, finely chopped
½ green chilli, finely chopped
4 slices prosciutto, finely chopped
1 × 400 g tin cannellini beans, drained and rinsed
½ cup chicken stock
1 tablespoon chopped flat-leaf (Italian) parsley
1 tablespoon chopped oregano

Heat oil in a large heavy-based saucepan over high
heat. Add spring onions, garlic and chilli and cook for
30 seconds. Add prosciutto and cook for a further minute.
Add beans and stir well, then add stock and bring to a
boil. Reduce heat and simmer for 5 minutes. Lightly crush
beans with a fork, then stir through the herbs.

　　Goes well with pork or chicken.

1 serve = 1 unit bread, 1 unit fats

white beans with spring onions & fresh herbs

cauliflower with leeks & parmesan

cauliflower with leeks
& parmesan

SIDES serves 4

1 tablespoon olive oil
1 leek, white part only, finely sliced and washed
3 cups small cauliflower florets
½ teaspoon nutmeg
2 cups low-fat milk
¼ cup grated parmesan

Heat oil in a large heavy-based saucepan over medium heat. Add leek and sauté for 5 minutes, or until soft. Add cauliflower, nutmeg and milk and bring to a boil. Reduce heat and simmer, covered, for 8 minutes, or until cauliflower is tender. Season lightly.

Heat grill to high. Drain cauliflower and leek mix and transfer to an ovenproof dish. Sprinkle with parmesan and place under grill until cheese is golden.

Goes well with beef, lamb or chicken.

1 serve = 1 unit vegetables, ½ unit dairy, 1 unit fats

pumpkin mash with cabbage
& spring onions

SIDES serves 4

2 tablespoons olive oil
500 g cabbage, finely shredded
600 g butternut pumpkin, peeled
    and cut into large chunks
1 cup low-fat milk
4 spring onions (scallions), finely sliced

Heat olive oil in a large frying pan over medium heat. Add cabbage and sauté for 5 minutes, or until soft. Remove from heat and set aside.

Fill a large saucepan with 2 cm lightly salted water and bring to a simmer. Add pumpkin, cover tightly, and cook for 15 minutes, or until tender. Drain well and return to pan. Add milk and mash pumpkin with a fork. To serve, season mash lightly and stir through cabbage and spring onions.

Goes well with beef or lamb.

1 serve = 2 units vegetables, 2 units fats

grilled eggplant with tomatoes & balsamic vinegar

SIDES serves 4

3 eggplants (aubergines), sliced into rounds
2 tablespoons olive oil
2 red (Spanish) onions, diced
2 cloves garlic, crushed
800 g tomatoes, diced
¼ cup roughly chopped mint
¼ cup roughly torn basil
2 tablespoons balsamic vinegar
1 tablespoon capers, chopped

Preheat a grill plate or barbecue grill to high. Lightly brush eggplant slices with half the oil, and season lightly. Grill for 2 minutes each side, or until browned. Transfer to a large mixing bowl and set aside.

Heat remaining oil in a large saucepan over high heat. Add onions and garlic and cook for 5 minutes, or until onions begin to soften. Add tomatoes and cook for a further 2 minutes. Season to taste. Pour tomato mixture over eggplant and add herbs, balsamic vinegar and capers. Carefully toss, and serve warm or cold.

Goes well with chicken or fish.

1 serve = 2 units vegetables, 2 units fats

roasted cherry tomatoes & asparagus with lemon thyme

SIDES serves 4

2 punnets cherry tomatoes
24 spears asparagus, cut into 6 cm pieces
1 tablespoon olive oil
1 tablespoon picked lemon thyme leaves
100 g rocket (arugula)

Preheat oven to 200°C (390°F).

Place tomatoes, asparagus, oil and thyme in a large bowl and mix well. Lightly season. Transfer to an ovenproof dish and bake for 10 minutes, or until tomatoes start to split. Remove from oven and toss vegetables through rocket. Serve immediately.

Goes well with lamb, pork, chicken or fish.

1 serve = 2 units vegetables, 1 unit fats

roasted cherry tomatoes and
asparagus with lemon thyme

For nights when you feel like a treat, try the following recipes. Although they sound naughty, they are well within the parameters of the CSIRO Total Wellbeing Diet.

desserts

baked apples with cinnamon & ricotta

Serves 4

2 large green apples
⅓ cup rolled oats
¼ cup mixed dried fruit
½ teaspoon ground cinnamon
½ cup low-fat ricotta
2 tablespoons maple syrup
400 g low-fat vanilla yoghurt

Preheat oven to 200°C (390°F).

Peel, core and halve apples and place, cut-side up, on a baking tray lined with baking paper. In a bowl, mix oats, dried fruit, cinnamon and ricotta. Spoon mixture into the core of each apple half, making a small mound. Drizzle with maple syrup and bake for 20 minutes. Serve warm with vanilla yoghurt.

1 serve = 1 unit dairy, 1 unit fruit

buttermilk puddings with fresh berries

Serves 6

1 vanilla bean, split
600 ml buttermilk
7 teaspoons powdered gelatine
¼ cup Equal or other powdered sweetener
250 ml low-fat vanilla yoghurt
600 g fresh seasonal berries (strawberries, raspberries, blueberries, etc.)

Place vanilla bean and half the buttermilk in a small saucepan and bring to a simmer. Remove from heat and add gelatine, stirring well to dissolve. Allow to cool slightly, stir in Equal, then strain through a fine-mesh sieve.

Place yoghurt and remaining buttermilk in a bowl and add vanilla yoghurt. Stir gently, then pour into 6 small ramekins or glasses. Refrigerate for 2 hours, or until set.

Serve puddings either in the ramekins or turned out onto plates, and with fresh berries.

1 serve = 1 unit dairy, 1 unit fruit

buttermilk puddings with fresh berries

spiced rhubarb & apple pie

spiced rhubarb & apple pie

Serves 4

1 teaspoon finely grated lemon zest
1 tablespoon lemon juice
¼ cup Equal or other powdered sweetener
2 teaspoons vanilla essence
½ teaspoon mixed spice
6 green apples, peeled, cored and quartered
1 cup apple juice
1 bunch rhubarb, cut into 4 cm pieces
1 quantity olive oil pastry (see below)
low-fat milk, for brushing

Preheat oven to 200°C (390°F).

Place lemon zest, lemon juice, Equal, vanilla essence, mixed spice, apples and apple juice into a large saucepan and bring to a boil. Reduce heat and simmer for 10 minutes, or until apple is soft but still holding its shape. Add rhubarb and cook for 2 minutes, or until rhubarb softens slightly. Remove from heat and pour into a shallow pie dish.

Roll out pastry to 5 mm thickness and the size of the pie dish. Brush rim of dish with a little milk, then drape pastry over, pressing the edges firmly onto the rim of the dish. Trim away excess pastry. Brush pastry lid with a little more milk and bake for 30 minutes, or until golden.

Serve warm with low-fat ice-cream or yoghurt, if desired.

1 serve = 1 unit bread, 2 units fruit, 2 units fats

olive oil pastry

Place 100 g wholemeal plain flour and a pinch of salt in a bowl. Add 2 tablespoons olive oil and rub into flour, using your fingers, until mixture resembles breadcrumbs. Sprinkle in 50 ml cold water, a little at a time, and mix together. Knead briefly, then set aside, covered with a clean tea towel, for 1 hour. Use as specified in recipe.

fruit bread pudding

Serves 4

3 teaspoons light margarine
8 slices wholegrain raisin bread, crusts removed
4 eggs
1 teaspoon vanilla essence
350 ml low-fat milk
2 teaspoons custard powder
2 tablespoons Equal or other powdered sweetener
250 g low-fat flavoured yoghurt

Preheat oven to 160°C (320°F).

Spread a little margarine on each slice of bread and cut slices in half. Layer bread on the bottom and sides of a small ovenproof dish.

In a bowl, whisk together eggs, vanilla, milk, custard powder and Equal, then pour mixture over bread. Leave to stand for 5 minutes to allow bread to absorb mixture. Place ovenproof dish in a deep baking dish and pour enough hot water into baking dish to come halfway up sides of pudding dish. Carefully transfer to oven and bake for 25 minutes, or until custard has set.

Serve warm, with low-fat yoghurt of your choice.

1 serve = ½ unit protein, 2 units bread,
1 unit dairy, ½ unit fats

passionfruit meringues with mango

Serves 6

6 egg whites
1 cup Equal or other powdered sweetener
2 passionfruit
1 teaspoon vanilla essence
1 teaspoon finely grated lemon zest
250 ml low-fat passionfruit yoghurt
500 g fresh mango, sliced

Preheat oven to 150°C (300°F). Line a baking tray with baking paper.

Place egg whites in a clean, dry bowl and, using a hand-held electric mixer, beat until soft peaks form. Gradually beat in Equal until mixture becomes stiff. Spoon mixture onto prepared baking tray in 6 equal-sized blobs and bake for 45 minutes, or until firm. Remove from oven and turn out onto a wire rack to cool.

Meanwhile, scoop passionfruit pulp into a bowl and stir in vanilla essence, lemon zest and yoghurt. Place meringues on serving plates, top with a dollop of passionfruit yoghurt and serve with fresh mango slices.

1 serve = ½ unit protein, 1 unit fruit

zabaglione

Serves 4

8 egg yolks
⅔ cup Equal or other powdered sweetener
1 teaspoon finely grated lemon zest
1 teaspoon vanilla essence
⅓ cup marsala
650 g stewed fruit

Half-fill a saucepan with water and bring to a boil, then reduce heat to a simmer. Place egg yolks and Equal in a heatproof bowl that will fit neatly on top of the saucepan, without touching the water. Using a hand-held electric mixer, lightly beat yolks. Position bowl on top of saucepan and continue to beat until yolks are pale and frothy. Add lemon zest and vanilla essence, and continue to beat while adding marsala a couple of drops at a time. When the mixture begins to resemble a soft, frothy cream, remove from heat.

To serve, pour zabaglione over stewed fruit.

1 serve = 1 unit protein, 1 unit fruit

zabaglione

baked banana with flaked almonds & grand marnier

Serves 6

½ teaspoon ground cardamom
juice and finely grated zest of 1 lemon
juice and finely grated zest of 1 orange
1 tablespoon Equal or other powdered sweetener
1 tablespoon maple syrup
¼ cup low-joule apricot jam
120 ml Grand Marnier
4 large bananas
2 tablespoons flaked almonds, toasted
500 g low-fat natural yoghurt

Preheat oven to 190°C (375°F). Lightly grease a medium-sized ovenproof dish.

Place cardamom, lemon juice and zest, orange juice and zest, Equal, maple syrup, apricot jam and Grand Marnier in a small saucepan. Bring to a simmer, then remove from heat and set aside.

Cut bananas into 3 cm pieces and place in prepared ovenproof dish. Pour warm syrup over bananas. Bake for 15 minutes, or until bananas are soft. Serve bananas sprinkled with almonds, and with yoghurt alongside.

1 serve = ½ unit dairy, 1 unit fruit

almond jelly with orange segments

Serves 6

450 ml boiling water
7 teaspoons powdered gelatine
375 ml light evaporated milk
1 teaspoon almond essence
2 teaspoons Equal or other powdered sweetener
6 oranges, segmented
¼ cup mint leaves

Pour water into a jug, add gelatine and whisk with a fork to dissolve. Add evaporated milk, almond essence and Equal, and mix well. Pour into 6 small ramekins, or other moulds, and refrigerate for 2 hours, or until set.

Before serving, toss orange segments with mint. Serve jellies either in the ramekins or turned out onto plates, and with orange segments.

1 serve = ½ unit dairy, 1 unit fruit

almond jelly with orange segments

appendices

APPENDIX 1

the CSIRO Total Wellbeing Diet checklist

week of diet:	Monday	Tuesday	Wednesday	Thursday	Friday	Saturday	Sunday
lean dinner protein (200 g)							
red meat 4 times a week							
fish twice a week							
other once a week							
lean lunch protein (up to 100 g)							
wholegrain bread (2 × 35 g slices)							
fruit (1 medium piece)							
fruit (1 medium piece)							
high-fibre cereal (1 serve)							
low-fat dairy (1 unit)							
low-fat dairy (1 unit)							
low-fat dairy (1 unit)							
salad (½ cup)							
vegetable 1 (½ cup)							
vegetable 2 (½ cup)							
vegetable 3 (½ cup)							
vegetable 4 (½ cup)							
oil or margarine (3 teaspoons)							
indulgence foods (2 units a week)							
other							
exercise (30 minutes)							

APPENDIX 2

maintenance checklist

Date:

week of maintenance plan:	Monday	Tuesday	Wednesday	Thursday	Friday	Saturday	Sunday
lean dinner protein (200 g)							
red meat 4 times a week							
fish twice a week							
other once a week							
lean lunch protein (up to 100 g)							
wholegrain bread (2 x 35 g slices)							
fruit (1 medium piece)							
fruit (1 medium piece)							
high-fibre cereal (1 serve)							
low-fat dairy (1 unit)							
low-fat dairy (1 unit)							
low-fat dairy (1 unit)							
salad (½ cup)							
vegetable 1 (½ cup)							
vegetable 2 (½ cup)							
vegetable 3 (½ cup)							
vegetable 4 (½ cup)							
oil or margarine (3 teaspoons)							
indulgence foods (2 units/week)							
500-kilojoule 'block'							
500-kilojoule 'block'							
500-kilojoule 'block'							
exercise (30 minutes)							

my training diary

Training week: ___

MY WORKOUT FOR THIS WEEK
I will complete my:
- aerobic walking program ___ times
- resistance tube training program ___ times
- warm-up and cool-down before and after each training session

AEROBIC WALKING PROGRAM
Training goals: ___ minutes a day, ___ times

day	time planned (mins)	time completed (mins)	distance covered (km)	comments
monday				
tuesday				
wednesday				
thursday				
friday				
saturday				
sunday				

Week's completed total: ___ minutes a day, ___ times

I achieved my weekly goals: yes/no

Goals for next week: _____

_____

_____

RESISTANCE TUBE TRAINING PROGRAM

Training goals: _____ repetitions per set, _____ sets per exercise

training completed		Monday			Tuesday			Wednesday			Thursday			Friday			Saturday			Sunday		
		set 1	set 2	set 3	set 1	set 2	set 3	set 1	set 2	set 3	set 1	set 2	set 3	set 1	set 2	set 3	set 1	set 2	set 3	set 1	set 2	set 3
1	lateral raises																					
2	squats with turned-out knees																					
	resisted squats																					
3	seated row																					
	standing row																					
4	chest press																					
5	lunges (each leg)																					
	resisted lunges (each leg)																					
6	lateral pull down																					
	upright row																					
7	triceps press																					
	arm press																					
8	biceps curls																					
9	crunches																					

Comments: _____

I achieved my weekly goals: yes/no

Goals for next week: _____

_____

_____

the CSIRO Total Wellbeing Diet progress chart

Use the chart below to graph your your progress from week to week.

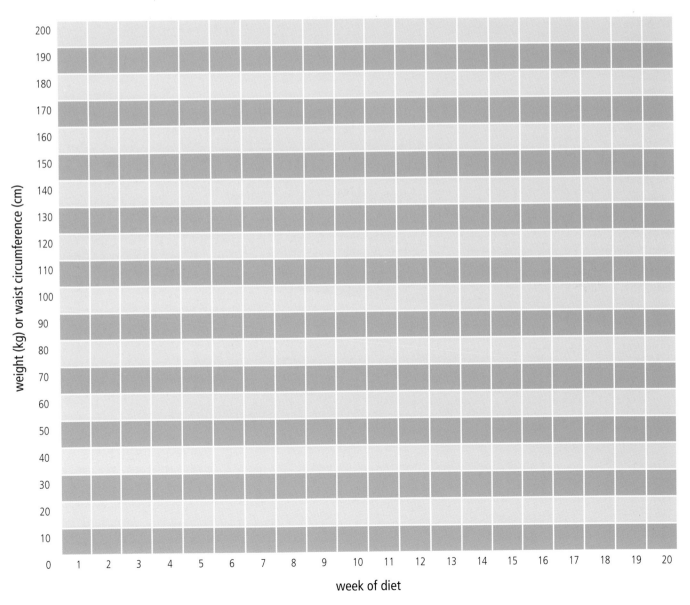

weight (kg) or waist circumference (cm)

week of diet

recommended daily vitamin and mineral intakes for adults**

vitamin/mineral	men			women				
	19–50 years	51–70 years	70+ years	19–50 years	51–70 years	70+ years	pregnant	breastfeed-ing
calcium (mg)	1000	1000	1300	1000	1300	1300	+0	+0
total folate (μg)	400	400	400	400	400	400	+200	+100
iodine (μg)	150	150	150	150	150	150	+70	+120
iron (mg)	8	8	8	18	8	8	+9	+9
magnesium (mg)	400–420	420	420	310–320	320	320	+30–40	+0
phosphorus (mg)	1000	1000	1000	1000	1000	1000	+0	+0
potassium* (mg)	3800	3800	3800	2800	2800	2800	+0	+400
selenium (μg)	70	70	70	60	60	60	+5	+15
sodium* (mg)	920–2300	920–2300	920–2300	920–2300	920–2300	920–2300	+0	+0
vitamin A (μg retinol equivalents)	900	900	900	700	700	700	+100	+400
vitamin B1 (thiamine) (mg)	1.2	1.2	1.2	1.1	1.1	1.1	+0.3	+0.3
vitamin B2 (riboflavin) (mg)	1.3	1.3	1.6	1.1	1.1	1.3	+0.3	+0.5
vitamin B3 (niacin) (mg niacin equivalents)	16	16	16	14	14	14	+4	+3
vitamin B6 (mg)	1.3	1.7	1.7	1.3	1.5	1.5	+0.6	+0.7
vitamin B12 (μg)	2.4	2.4	2.4	2.4	2.4	2.4	+0.2	+0.4
vitamin C (mg)	45	45	45	45	45	45	+15	+40
vitamin E* (mg alpha-tocopherol equivalents)	10	10	10	7	7	7	+0	+4
zinc (mg)	14	14	14	8	8	8	+3	+4

*   The National Health and Medical Research Council does not offer recommended daily intakes for these nutrients: the figures for potassium and vitamin E indicate an adequate level of intake; those for sodium give a range from adequate intake to the recommended upper level of intake

** Data copyright © Commonwealth Government of Australia 2006, reproduced by permission

shopping lists

These shopping lists cover all the foods used in the menu plans on pages 75–99. Use the lists if you are following the menu plans exactly, or alter them slightly if you have personalised the plans to include your favourite foods. 'In the cupboard or fridge' is a list of common ingredients used in the menu plans. You will need these ingredients to follow the menu plans, but most are cooking staples, and you may already have many of them.

In the cupboard or fridge . . .

fruit (tinned)
dried fruit (apples, currants,
    mixed, sultanas)
almonds
pine nuts
frozen peas
frozen spinach
onions (brown, red)
potatoes
garlic
ginger
eggs
low-fat milk
low-fat flavoured yoghurt
dairy desserts (low-fat custard,
    low-fat ice-cream, etc.)
wholegrain bread
wholegrain bread rolls
wholegrain crispbreads
wholemeal breadcrumbs
breakfast cereals (including
    high-fibre cereal, oats)
rolled oats
untoasted muesli
unprocessed wheatbran
couscous
polenta
rice (basmati, brown, long-grain)

anchovy fillets
capers (including baby)
balsamic vinegar
white-wine vinegar
flour (plain and self-raising,
    including wholemeal)
cornflour
sugar (brown, white)
Equal or other powdered sweetener
cocoa
vanilla essence
low-joule vegetable soup
salt-reduced stock (beef, chicken, fish, vegetable)
spices (black pepper – cracked, freshly ground,
    peppercorns; cardamom – ground & pods;
    cayenne pepper; chilli powder;
    garam masala; Chinese five-spice powder;
    cinnamon – ground & sticks; cloves;
    coriander – ground & seeds; cumin – ground;
    curry powder; fennel – ground; lemon pepper;
    turmeric; nutmeg – ground; paprika;
    white pepper)
dried herbs (bay leaves, oregano, mixed)
white sesame seeds
tinned fish (tuna, salmon)
light margarine
low-joule jam
honey
Vegemite

mustard (Dijon, powder, wholegrain)
oil-free mayonnaise
oil-free salad dressing (including balsamic)
horseradish
tomato sauce
Worcestershire sauce
tomato paste
tinned tomatoes
baked beans
light coconut milk
tandoori paste
pesto (basil, sun-dried tomato)
chutney (including spicy mango)
pickles
gherkins
redcurrant jelly
apple sauce
cranberry sauce
plum sauce
cooking oil (canola, peanut, sesame)
olive oil (light, extra-virgin)
olive oil spray
soy sauce (dark, light)
oyster sauce
hoisin sauce
sweet chilli sauce
dry sherry (or Chinese rice wine)
fish sauce
orange juice
wine (red, white)

These weekly shopping lists and the 'In the cupboard or fridge' list will provide you with all you need for the 12-week menu plans. The quantities needed will depend on how many people in the household are on the Diet, how many are on the basic plan and whether they eat the suggested main meals. Copy the lists and fill in the quantities or download them with quantities from www.csiro.au/twd.

week one

fresh fruit (including bananas, green apples, lemons, limes, seasonal fruit)
asparagus
avocado
bean sprouts
broccoli
capsicums (red, yellow)
carrots
chillies (small red)
herbs (basil, coriander, mint, flat-leaf parsley, Thai basil, lemon thyme, thyme)
mixed vegetables (for salad, steaming)
pumpkin (butternut)
salad leaves (mixed-leaf, rocket)
snow pea sprouts
spring onions
tomatoes (including cherry)
zucchini
sardines
calamari
white fish fillets
skinless chicken breast fillets, and drumsticks and thighs on the bone
sliced turkey
roast pork
rump steaks and sirloin
lamb chops and lean minced lamb
feta
low-fat ricotta
low-fat yoghurt (natural, vanilla)
maple syrup

week two

fresh fruit (including lemons, limes)
avocado
bean sprouts
bok choy
broccolini
Brussels sprouts
carrots
cauliflowers
chillies (green, large red)
corn
cucumbers
fennel
green beans
herbs (coriander, lemongrass, kaffir lime leaves, flat-leaf parsley)
mixed vegetables (for salad)
mushrooms (button)
peas
pumpkin
squash
tomatoes
salad leaves (mixed-leaf, rocket, baby spinach)
spring onions
salmon fillets
white fish fillets
skinless chicken breast fillets
sliced turkey
sliced lean ham
beef fillets and lean strips
veal loin
lamb leg steaks
cheddar cheese
low-fat natural yoghurt
cashews
olives (kalamata, pitted green)

week three

fresh fruit (including fruit salad, lemons, limes, oranges)
avocado
bok choy
broccoli
broccolini
capsicums (red)
carrots (including baby)
chillies (red, green)
corn
cucumbers
green beans (including baby)
herbs (basil, coriander, mint, flat-leaf parsley, rosemary, thyme)
mixed vegetables (for salad)
mushrooms (large flat)
parsnips (small)
peas
pumpkin (including butternut)
salad leaves (mixed-leaf, rocket, baby spinach)
snow peas
spring onions
tomatoes (including Roma)
blue-eye trevalla fillets
white fish fillets
skinless chicken breast fillets
lean bacon, pork cutlets and sliced lean ham
beef fillets and sirloin
veal cutlets
lamb leg and lean minced lamb
cheddar cheese
cottage cheese
low-fat natural yoghurt
tinned baby beetroot

week four

fresh fruit (including fruit salad, lemons, limes)
avocado
bean sprouts
broccolini
carrots
celery
chillies (large red)
cucumbers
eggplants
fennel
green beans
herbs (basil, coriander, lemongrass, kaffir lime leaves, mint, oregano, flat-leaf parsley, rosemary, thyme)
leeks
mixed vegetables (for salad)
parsnips
peas
pumpkin
salad leaves (mixed-leaf, rocket, baby spinach)
spring onions
squash
tomatoes (including cherry)
zucchini
tinned crab meat
smoked salmon
fish fillets (blue-eye, flathead or ling)
salmon fillets
sliced lean ham
skinless chicken breast fillets
lean topside roast and rump steaks
lamb fillets and lean minced lamb
cheddar cheese (low- and full-fat)
low-fat ricotta
wholemeal Lebanese flatbreads
burghul
olives
tinned corn (or corn cobs)

week five

fresh fruit (including fruit salad, green apples, lemons, limes, seasonal fruit)
asparagus
avocado
bean sprouts
bok choy (baby)
broccoli
cabbage
capsicums (red)
carrots
cauliflower
chillies (green, large red, small red)
cucumbers (Lebanese)
fennel
green beans
herbs (coriander, mint, flat-leaf parsley, rosemary, Thai basil)
lettuce (baby cos)
mixed vegetables (for salad)
pumpkin (butternut)
salad leaves (mixed-leaf, watercress)
snow peas
snow pea sprouts
spinach
spring onions
tomatoes
zucchini
calamari
salmon steaks
skinless chicken breast and thigh fillets
sliced turkey
roast pork
lean beef (for curry) and lean minced beef
lamb chops and fillets, and lean minced lamb
low-fat cheddar cheese
low-fat feta
Swiss cheese
low-fat natural yoghurt
rye bread
rigatoni
low-fat hummus
olives (green)
red miso paste

week six

fresh fruit (including fruit salad, green apples, lemons, limes, seasonal fruit)
avocado
bok choy (baby)
broccoli
carrots
cauliflower
celery
chillies (green)
cucumbers
green beans
herbs (basil, coriander, flat-leaf parsley, rosemary, lemon thyme)
mixed vegetables (for salad)
mushrooms (button, Swiss brown, oyster, shiitake)
pumpkin (including butternut)
salad leaves (mixed-leaf, baby spinach)
spinach
spring onions
squash
tomatoes
ocean trout fillets
tuna steaks
skinless chicken breast fillets, and drumsticks and thighs on the bone
sliced lean ham and roast pork
lean beef strips and rump steaks
lamb fillets and shoulder
cheddar cheese
parmesan
low-fat natural yoghurt
wholemeal Lebanese flatbreads
black sesame seeds
marinated artichoke hearts
pitted dates

week seven

fresh fruit (including apples,
    fruit salad, lemons, limes)
avocado
bean sprouts
bok choy
broccoli
capsicums (red, yellow)
carrots
cauliflower
chillies (green, large red, small red)
corn
cucumbers
eggplants
green beans
herbs (coriander, lemongrass,
    kaffir lime leaves, mint, oregano,
    flat-leaf parsley, rosemary, thyme)
leeks
mixed vegetables (for salad)
mushrooms (button)
peas
pumpkin
salad leaves (mixed-leaf, rocket)
spring onions
tomatoes (including Roma)
zucchini
prawns
salmon fillets
sardines
skinless chicken breast fillets,
    and drumsticks and thighs
    on the bone
sliced turkey
lean bacon and sliced lean ham
beef fillets and rump steaks
lamb chops and lean minced lamb
low-fat cheddar cheese
low-fat ricotta
parmesan
wholemeal Lebanese flatbreads
wholemeal pita bread
chick peas (tinned or cooked)
olives
tinned three-bean mix

week eight

fresh fruit (including fruit salad, lemons)
bok choy (baby)
broccolini
carrots
chillies (large red)
cucumbers
eggplants
fennel
herbs (coriander, mint, flat-leaf parsley)
mixed vegetables (for salad)
peas
salad leaves (mixed-leaf, rocket,
    baby spinach)
snow peas
spring onions
squash (including baby)
tomatoes
zucchini
bream fillets
white fish fillets
skinless chicken breast
    and thigh fillets
sliced lean ham
pastrami
lean minced beef
veal loin
lamb leg and lean minced lamb
wholemeal crumpets
wholemeal pita bread
cheddar cheese
parmesan
Swiss cheese
low-fat natural yoghurt
low-fat hummus
chick peas (tinned or cooked)
kalamata olives
tomato passata (tomato purée)

week nine

fresh fruit (including fruit salad, lemons)
asparagus
avocado
bok choy
broccoli
capsicums (red)
carrots
celery
corn
fennel
herbs (basil, flat-leaf parsley,
    rosemary, lemon thyme, thyme)
leeks
mixed vegetables (for salad)
peas
pumpkin
salad leaves (mixed-leaf, rocket,
    baby spinach)
snow peas
spring onions
squash
tomatoes (including cherry)
zucchini
fish fillets (blue-eye, flathead or ling)
white fish fillets
skinless chicken breast fillets
sliced lean ham and sliced prosciutto
pastrami
sirloin
veal cutlets
lamb chops and lean minced lamb
cheddar cheese
feta
low-fat ricotta
rye bread
wholemeal Lebanese flatbreads
caraway seeds
pickled onions
Sichuan pepper

week ten

fresh fruit (including fruit salad, green apples, lemons, limes, oranges, seasonal fruit)
avocado
bok choy (baby)
Brussels sprouts
capsicums (red)
carrots
cauliflower
chillies (green)
cucumbers
herbs (basil, coriander, flat-leaf parsley)
mixed vegetables (for salad)
mushrooms (Swiss brown, oyster, shiitake)
peas
pumpkin
salad leaves (mixed-leaf, baby spinach, watercress)
snow peas
spinach
spring onions
squash
tomatoes
zucchini
blue-eye trevalla fillets
ocean trout fillets
sardines
skinless chicken breast fillets
sliced roast beef
sirloin and lean minced beef
lamb leg steaks and shoulder
cheddar cheese (full- and low-fat)
feta (full- and low-fat)
low-fat natural yoghurt
rye bread
rigatoni
black sesame seeds
pitted dates

week eleven

fresh fruit (including fruit salad, lemons, limes)
avocado
bok choy
broccoli
broccolini
carrots
chillies (green)
cucumbers
green beans (including baby)
herbs (basil, coriander, flat-leaf parsley)
mixed vegetables (for salad)
parsnips (small)
salad leaves (mixed-leaf, rocket, baby spinach)
snow peas
spinach
spring onions
squash (baby)
tomatoes
zucchini
bream fillets
white fish fillets
skinless chicken breast fillets
sliced turkey
roast pork
lean beef (for curry) and beef fillets
veal cutlets
lamb leg steaks
feta
goat's cheese
low-fat cheddar cheese
Swiss cheese
low-fat natural yoghurt
wholemeal Lebanese flatbreads
cashews
olives (pitted green)
tinned corn
tinned three-bean mix

week twelve

fresh fruit (including fruit salad, green apples, lemons, limes, seasonal fruit)
avocado
bean sprouts
bok choy (baby)
broccoli
broccolini
carrots
capsicums (red)
chillies (green, red)
cucumbers
green beans
herbs (basil, coriander, mint, flat-leaf parsley, rosemary, sage)
mixed vegetables (for salad)
mushrooms (Swiss brown, oyster, shiitake)
peas
pumpkin
salad leaves (mixed-leaf, baby spinach)
spring onions
squash
tomatoes (including Roma)
zucchini
smoked salmon
ocean trout fillets
white fish fillets
skinless chicken breast fillets
pork loin
rump steaks
lamb chops, fillets and leg
buttermilk
low-fat cheddar cheese
feta
parmesan
low-fat natural yoghurt
wholemeal pita bread
black sesame seeds
marinated artichoke hearts
tinned corn (or corn cobs)

evidence for the effectiveness of higher-protein diets

Higher-protein diets for weight management have been investigated in several trials. The benefits go well beyond how much weight is lost. The key benefits are that higher-protein diets provide more nutrients, and they have been shown to improve body composition, assist in appetite control and lower blood fats called triglycerides to a greater degree than high-carbohydrate diets. These conclusions arise both from our own studies (see below) and those of researchers overseas.

Bowen, J., Noakes, M. & Clifton, P.M. Appetite regulatory hormone responses to various dietary proteins differ by BMI status despite similar reductions in ad libitum energy intake. *Journal of Clinical Endocrinology & Metabolism* 2006, published online 30 May.

Bowen, J., Noakes, M. & Clifton, P.M. Effect of calcium and dairy foods in high-protein, energy-restricted diets on weight loss and metabolic parameters in overweight adults. *International Journal of Obesity* 2005, 29(8): 957–65.

Bowen, J., Noakes, M. & Clifton, P.M. Effects of dietary protein type on energy intake and appetite regulatory hormones. *Asia Pacific Journal of Clinical Nutrition 2005*, 14(Suppl.): S66.

Bowen, J., Noakes, M., Trenerry, C. & Clifton, P.M. Energy intake, ghrelin, and cholecystokinin after different carbohydrate and protein preloads in overweight men. *Journal of Clinical Endocrinology & Metabolism* 2006, 91(4): 1477–83.

Brinkworth, G.D., Noakes, M., Parker, B., Foster, P. & Clifton, P.M. Long term effects of advice to consume a high-protein, low-fat diet, rather than a conventional weight-loss diet, in obese adults with type 2 diabetes: one-year follow-up of a randomised trial. *Diabetologia* 2004, 47(10): 1677–86.

Clifton, P.M., Keogh, J.B., Foster, P.R. & Noakes, M. Effect of weight loss on inflammatory and endothelial markers and FMD using two low-fat diets. *International Journal of Obesity* 2005, 29(12): 1445–51.

Farnsworth, E., Luscombe, N.D., Noakes, M., Wittert, G., Argyiou, E. & Clifton, P.M. Effect of a high-protein, energy-restricted diet on body composition, glycemic control, and lipid concentrations in overweight and obese hyperinsulinemic men and women. *American Journal of Clinical Nutrition* 2003, 78(1): 31–9.

Keogh, J.B., Grieger, J.A., Noakes, M. & Clifton, P.M. Flow-mediated dilatation is impaired by a high-saturated fat diet but not by a high-carbohydrate diet. *Arteriosclerosis, Thrombosis, and Vascular Biology* 2005, 25(6): 1274–9.

Luscombe-Marsh, N.D., Noakes, M., Wittert, G.A., Keogh, J.B., Foster, P. & Clifton, P.M. Carbohydrate-restricted diets high in either monounsaturated fat or protein are equally effective at promoting fat loss and improving blood lipids. *American Journal of Clinical Nutrition* 2005, 81(4): 762–72.

Moran, L.J., Brinkworth, G., Noakes, M. & Norman, R.J. Effects of lifestyle modification in polycystic ovarian syndrome. *Reproductive BioMedicine Online* 2006, 12(5): 569–78.

Moran, L.J., Luscombe-Marsh, N., Noakes, M., Wittert, G.A., Keogh, J.B. & Clifton, P.M. The satiating effect of dietary protein is unrelated to post-prandial ghrelin secretion. *Asia Pacific Journal of Clinical Nutrition* 2005, 14(Suppl.): S64.

Moran, L.J., Luscombe-Marsh, N.D., Noakes, M., Wittert, G.A., Keogh, J.B. & Clifton, P.M. The satiating effect of dietary protein is unrelated to post-prandial ghrelin secretion. *Journal of Clinical Endocrinology & Metabolism* 2005, published online 12 July.

Moran, L.J., Noakes, M., Clifton, P.M., Wittert, G.A., Williams, G. & Norman, R.J. Short-term meal replacements followed by dietary macronutrient restriction enhance weight loss in polycystic ovary syndrome. *American Journal of Clinical Nutrition* 2006, 84(1): 77–87.

Moran, L.J., Noakes, M., Clifton, P.M., Wittert, G.A., Williams, G. & Norman, R.J. Effective weight loss and maintenance strategies in polycystic ovary syndrome. *Asia Pacific Journal of Clinical Nutrition* 2005, 14(Suppl.): S94.

Noakes, M. & Clifton, P. Weight loss, diet composition and cardiovascular risk. *Current Opinion in Lipidology* 2004, 15(1): 31–5.

Noakes, M., Bowen J. & Clifton, P. Dairy foods or fractions for appetite and weight control. *Australian Journal of Dairy Technology* 2005, 60(2): 152–3.

Noakes, M., Lau, C.W.H., Bowen, J. & Clifton, P.M. The effect of a low glycaemic index (GI) ingredient substituted for a high GI ingredient in two complete meals on blood glucose and insulin levels, satiety and energy intake in healthy lean women. *Asia Pacific Journal of Clinical Nutrition* 2005, 14(Suppl.): S45.

Noakes, M., Foster, P.R., Keogh, J.B. & Clifton, P.M. Post prandial glucose and insulin responses to test meals and insulin sensitivity after weight loss on a very low carbohydrate diet compared to low fat high carbohydrate diets. *Asia Pacific Journal of Clinical Nutrition* 2005, 14(Suppl.): S112.

Noakes, M., Foster, P.R., Keogh, J.B., James, A.P., Mamo, J.C. & Clifton, P.M. Comparison of isocaloric very low carbohydrate/high saturated fat and high carbohydrate/low saturated fat diets on body composition and cardiovascular risk. *Nutrition & Metabolism* 2006, 3(1): 7.

Noakes, M., Keogh, J.B., Foster, P.R. & Clifton, P.M. Effect of an energy-restricted, high-protein, low-fat diet relative to a conventional high-carbohydrate, low-fat diet on weight loss, body composition, nutritional status, and markers of cardiovascular health in obese women. *American Journal of Clinical Nutrition* 2005, 81(6): 1298–1306.

Noakes, M., Williams, G., Keogh, J.B. & Clifton, P.M. Influence of high protein snack foods on satiety, food intake and glucose and insulin response: a single blind cross over study. *Asia Pacific Journal of Clinical Nutrition* 2005, 14(Suppl.): S113.

Parker, B., Noakes, M., Luscombe, N. & Clifton, P. Effect of a high-protein, high-monounsaturated fat weight loss diet on glycemic control and lipid levels in type 2 diabetes. *Diabetes Care* 2002, 25(3): 425–30.

index